'A treasure trove of ideas for the new working world.'

Jo Youle, Chief Executive, Missing People

'A masterful and stimulating read. A practical book full of ideas for modern leaders who embrace the change.'

Gosia Walendzik, Founder, Medica Assistance

'In this excellent book on leadership, Jo brings a lifetime of work and his trademark pragmatism to one of the most important issues for all leaders today – how to help their teams be the best they can be while working remotely.'

David Stephen, Group Chief Risk Officer, Westpac

'*Smart Work* combines powerful insights into some of the factors that have led teams and organizations to thrive, struggle, or both through realities of the pandemic, with provocations for how we can learn from this time to harness the power of what we've realised is now possible.'

Emily Preston, Senior Project Lead, Innovation Unit

'The new era of hybrid working has just begun: in this book, you can already find effective solutions to stay ahead of the game in the next years.'

Marco Maccari, Head of HR Talent & Rewards, Fater

SMART WORK

The Ultimate Handbook for Remote and Hybrid Teams

JO OWEN

BLOOMSBURY BUSINESS
LONDON • OXFORD • NEW YORK • NEW DELHI • SYDNEY

BLOOMSBURY BUSINESS
Bloomsbury Publishing Plc
50 Bedford Square, London, WC1B 3DP, UK
29 Earlsfort Terrace, Dublin 2, Ireland

BLOOMSBURY, BLOOMSBURY BUSINESS and the Diana logo are
trademarks of Bloomsbury Publishing Plc

First published in Great Britain 2021

A catalogue record for this book is available from the British Library

Library of Congress Cataloguing-in-Publication data has been applied for

ISBN: 978-1-4729-9252-9; eBook: 978-1-4729-9251-2

2 4 6 8 10 9 7 5 3 1

Typeset by Deanta Global Publishing Services, Chennai, India
Printed and bound in Great Britain by CPI Group (UK) Ltd, Croydon
CR0 4YY

To find out more about our authors and books visit www.bloomsbury.com
and sign up for our newsletters

Contents

Preface   vii

Summary   ix

Introduction: the Smart Work challenge   1

**1   Relationships: build networks of trust and
       support to make things happen**   13

    1.0   The nature of the hybrid working revolution   14
    1.1   Build values alignment   20
    1.2   Find goals alignment   28
    1.3   Demonstrate credibility   34
    1.4   Manage risk   40
    1.5   Create your network of influence   44
    1.6   Key points   50

2   Autonomy and accountability to drive action   53

    2.0   The autonomy and accountability challenge   53
    2.1   Managing professionals remotely: managing
        better by managing less   54
    2.2   Recrafting your role as a leader in a world of
        high autonomy   59
    2.3   Driving change and sustaining the revolution   63
    2.4   Key points   72

3   Motivation, mental health and mastery to sustain high performance   75

  3.0   Motivation and the mental health challenge
       of WFH   75
  3.1   Create the conditions in which you and your
       team will thrive   77
  3.2   Manage your inner world to sustain your health
       and performance   81
  3.3   Motivate yourself and your team   88
  3.4   Key points   114

4   Process: fix the plumbing of remote working   117

  4.1   Set yourself up for success   118
  4.2   Set your team up for success   127
  4.3   Create the rhythms and routines of success   137
  4.4   Create your team's own unique success formula   140
  4.5   Collaborate remotely: presentations, workshops
       and conferences   146
  4.6   Make meetings work   153
  4.7   Key points   175

Conclusion: the new world of Smart Work   177
Acknowledgements   183
Index   184

Preface: Smart Work

I started work on this book, by accident, nearly 20 years ago. When we started Teach First, which is now the UK's largest graduate recruiter, we had to develop a leadership programme at zero cost because we had no money. Suddenly, I had to find out what leadership was all about. Since then, I have been exploring leadership in every context, industry and continent. I have worked with over 100 of the best, and a couple of the worst, organizations on our planet. The research has taken in global businesses, micro-businesses, entrepreneurs, NGOs, sports teams, explorers and special forces. I have spent more time than is wise exploring how traditional societies lead and manage themselves. I have even seen how the nuclear deterrent at sea is managed.

The original research for this book included revisiting many of the organizations I had worked with or studied before. In every case, it was clear that the coronavirus pandemic has been a game changer.

The result is a book deliberately short on theory. It focuses on what is working in practice around the world and in hugely varied organizations. This book outlines best practice on all the practical challenges of Smart Work, and shows how you can design a solution tailor-made to your needs. It explores:

- How to split time and work between home and office.
- How to communicate and co-ordinate remotely.

- How to build the correct IT structure to support remote working.
- How to have effective meetings.
- How to manage time and workloads.
- How to sustain intrinsic motivation when working remotely.
- How to deal with stress and burnout.
- How to achieve some work-life balance.
- How to manage the conflicting needs of different employees and different types of work: not all work and not all staff are suited to hybrid or remote working.

Changing office routines, technology and operations is relatively simple. Changing skills and styles of leadership is far harder. This book will show you how and why leadership and management is changing in the world of hybrid teams. It will also show you how you can turn risk into opportunity: you will discover how you can thrive in the new world of twenty-first-century leadership and work.

Summary

The original research for this book was both global and, appropriately, remote. The challenges and solutions from around the world, across industries and from small to large firms, varied hugely in detail. But they all fitted into a broad and consistent framework: RAMP.

RAMP stands for:

1. Relationships: build networks of trust and support to make things happen.
2. Autonomy and accountability to drive action.
3. Motivation, mental health and mastery to sustain peak performance.
4. Process: fix the plumbing of remote working.

RAMP shows how you can rise to the challenge of hybrid working as a leader, manager or team member. *Smart Work* is organized into four chapters covering each element of RAMP.

1 Relationships: build networks of trust and support to make things happen

During the early stages of the pandemic, the loss of face-to-face relationships helped us discover how much we value them. This matters for morale, motivation and effectiveness. No one can succeed alone. You have to make things happen through other people. You need your networks of trust, support and influence.

In the office, you can build these networks naturally through the endless spontaneous chats which happen every day. Working remotely, it is much harder to build those networks of trust and support. Many people have found that they succeeded because they were able to draw on their existing pool of trust and support, forged when everyone was in the office together. But the longer teams stay remote, the more that trust starts to fray. New team members in particular find it hard to build the relationships they need to succeed.

Leaders and team members face the same challenge: how do I build and maintain my network of trust and support? For leaders, the challenge is particularly acute: remote working requires far more trust than working in the office. In the office you can see who is doing what. Even if

No one can succeed alone

you are not a micromanager, you can stay in control simply by looking and listening. When your team is working remotely, you do not even know what they are wearing beneath the waistline. You cannot really tell how hard they are working. You have to trust them to do the right things while you are not watching. It is a huge test of trust for the leader and of values for the team member.

Fortunately, you can learn how to build networks of trust and support. The four keys to trust are:

- *Align goals*. It is hard to trust someone who has conflicting goals. Teams only work well when they have a common goal.
- *Align values*. It is far easier to trust someone who shares similar values, experiences, ways of communicating and thinking. Getting to know colleagues is not a waste of time; it is an investment of time in building trust.
- *Build credibility*. We all have friends we like but we may not trust them: we know that they may be great

company but they might not always be reliable. Professionals are normally reliable: they do as they say. The challenge is rarely in the doing, it is in the saying. What we say and what is heard can be very different things. Miscommunication is the rust in trust and it is often fatal.

- *Manage risk.* Risk is analogue, not digital. More risk requires more trust. And real risk is not rational, but instead is more political and emotional: how will this affect me, my work, my bonus and my career?

All four of these keys to trust require seeing the world through the eyes of your colleagues. That in turn means that you need the secret characteristic of all the best leaders and sales people: they have two ears and one mouth, and they use them in that proportion. Listening and asking smart questions is far more effective than talking and making smart comments.

All the best leaders and sales people have two ears and one mouth

2 Autonomy and accountability to drive action

Chapter 2 shows how you can rise to the challenges of action, autonomy and accountability.

Professionals have always craved autonomy and resisted micromanagement. The pandemic turned autonomy from a 'nice to have' into a 'must-have'. It is far harder to micromanage people you can neither oversee nor overhear.

But autonomy is never a free lunch. More autonomy marches hand in hand with more accountability. Accountability and autonomy are a challenge for team leaders, team members and for how you can make things happen.

- *The leader's challenge*: leading more and managing less. In remote working, leaders have to learn to delegate more and better. You have to trust your team more because you cannot control them so closely. But the more you delegate, the more you need to know where you really make a difference as a leader. If you delegate everything, what is left for you? In practice, what is left is the essence of leadership:
  - Come up with an idea or plan to take your team where it would not have got by itself.
  - Select, develop, manage and motivate your team to make it happen.
  - Find the money, resources and political support to help your team succeed.

  Remote working forces you as a leader to focus on where you make the most difference as a leader. It makes you raise your game even further.

- *The team member's challenge*: balancing autonomy and accountability. There are three keys to success in finding this balance:
  - Manage your work-life balance. Remote working destroyed boundaries between work and life. You have to regain control of your life. Build appropriate boundaries so that you can work productively and rest properly. Learn how to manage your energy levels to sustain performance for the long term.
  - Set yourself up for success. Make sure you have the right goals with the right support.
  - Demonstrate performance. When working remotely it is not enough to have a claim to fame, because no one will know about it. You have to stake your claim to fame, without alienating everyone by playing politics and stealing the

limelight from colleagues who may also deserve credit for their work.

- *The action challenge*: sustaining change, not just sustaining the status quo. Autonomy and accountability are pointless unless they lead to action and results. The start of the pandemic saw firms and teams achieve more progress in four weeks than many had seen in four years. But remote working has proven to be better suited to managing the status quo than it is to managing change. Leaders and team members can draw on the experience of the pandemic to learn how you can deliver radical change at high speed. If you create the right conditions, change is always possible on remote and in-person teams.

3 Motivation, mental health and mastery to sustain peak performance

Chapter 3 explores how you can create the conditions where your team sustains its own intrinsic motivation, and how you can help your team develop the mastery it needs to sustain high performance.

Sadly, there is a silent epidemic of mental ill health as a result of the pandemic. Social animals do not thrive in isolation. When working remotely, you have to learn to look after your mental health, and – where possible – to tame your internal chatter. Fortunately, there is a series of mental habits that can be learned by everyone, and which convert your internal chatter from being destructive to constructive.

As a team leader, you cannot hope to be a psychiatrist to your team members. Nor can you simply tell your team to be motivated or happy: that will not motivate them. If you find yourself trying to motivate a demotivated team, something is wrong. Instead, create the right conditions and your team will motivate themselves. If a team member is demotivated, there is either something wrong with their working conditions or with the team member themselves. Their working conditions are deeply affected by the way you behave, either as a boss or colleague.

You cannot simply tell your team to be motivated or happy

There are a series of routines you can adopt to help your team discover their intrinsic motivation and maintain their mental health. These routines are captured in another version of the RAMP formula. Here is what it covers:

- *Supportive relationships* are vital: do not suffer alone. And if you are to succeed, you cannot succeed alone. Lone heroes exist in the movies, but, in real life, success is a team effort. This is a paradigm shift: leaders have to move from controlling to supporting their teams, especially as remote working makes command and control harder than ever.
- *Autonomy* only works if you know how to control it. If you do not control it, autonomy becomes a recipe for overwork, loss of work-life balance, stress and burnout. To make the most of autonomy you need to:
  ◦ Have clear goals, both long term and short term.
  ◦ Create clear boundaries between work and life.
  ◦ Develop daily rhythms and routines which allow you to sustain your energy and maximize your performance.
- *Mastery* matters because, if you have autonomy, you need to be confident that you have the skills to perform. Autonomy without mastery leads to disaster. The challenge for hybrid teams is how you can continue to grow and hone your skills when you are not with your colleagues. You can refresh explicit or technical skills

relatively easily with the profusion of online courses. But you also need to grow your tacit or 'know-how' skills, which are at least as important as your 'know-what' explicit skills. The Mastery section will show how you can keep on learning and keep on building your own unique success formula which works in your current job.

- *Purpose* drives motivation. We all do better when we feel we are part of something bigger than ourselves. Purpose rarely comes from corporate mission statements, and few people jump out of bed hoping to improve the firm's earnings per share. As a team leader, the trick is to craft your job so that it has personal **Success is a team effort** purpose and meaning. The Purpose section will show how you can craft any job to achieve that goal.

4 Process: fix the plumbing of remote working

Chapter 4 not only shows what good processes and routines look like. It also shows you how you can create a process that enables your team to continually improve its practices and performance. Change and improvement are not one-off events: they are part of a continual process.

The paradox of plumbing is that no one cares about it, or even thinks about it, until it goes wrong. And then everyone points the finger at everyone else, no one wants to get dirty sorting it out, and suddenly there is a crisis. You have to set yourself up for success, so get the plumbing of your remote team right from the start.

The good news is that the pandemic forced firms to focus on the mechanics of working remotely, which in turn means that best practices are fairly well established. Chapter 4 will highlight the best practices that deal with the most common challenges and questions raised by hybrid and remote working:

- How can we establish productive team rhythms and routines for working?
- How can we tame the communications beast?
- What sort of work should we do remotely and what should happen in the office?
- Do we need the office, and if so what should it look like?
- How can we set people up at home so that they can work productively?
- Who needs to be in the office, and who should work from home and when?
- How can we avoid doom by Zoom?
- What technology do we need?
- What needs to be different about online presentations and conferences to make them work?
- How can we make online team meetings productive?

Before the pandemic, many of these questions seemed to pose impossible challenges. Now, they are relatively routine questions of process and plumbing. You will not win by getting it right, but you will struggle mightily if you get it wrong.

Introduction: the Smart Work challenge

The COVID-19 pandemic which began in 2020 has forced the greatest shift in management and leadership practice for over 200 years. The old ways of leading by command and control were forged in the Industrial Revolution in order to control and manage hordes of workers, but what worked then was never going to be effective for leading highly paid professionals who work remotely. The pandemic has forced leadership to move from the nineteenth century to the twenty-first century. Those changes were coming anyway – the pandemic merely hastened their arrival.

We are now in a new world of work. The changes brought about by the pandemic were not temporary, but a completely new paradigm shift. We can no more go back to the old ways of working than we can uninvent computers and the internet. The pandemic revealed three changes in the nature of work and leadership:

1. Firms, teams and leaders can change and adapt faster than we ever thought possible.
2. Remote working raises the bar for leaders, managers and team members.
3. Hybrid working is finally bringing leadership into the twenty-first century.

Teams, leaders and firms that learn the lessons and are able to sustain the pace of change will flourish. Those who hope that they have 'done' change and settle into a quiet life of the new normal will soon find that they fall far behind. Comfort zones become uncomfortable for those that do not change.

As with all revolutions, the pandemic caused immense suffering. But like all revolutions it has challenged our assumptions about how things are and how they should be. The world is now in a markedly different place. For leaders, managers and teams,

Comfort zones become uncomfortable for those that do not change

it can be in a far better place than before. This book is your guide to adapting and succeeding in the new world of work.

Welcome to *Smart Work*.

The three great paradigm shifts of Smart Work

The shift to Smart Work is a great opportunity and risk for everyone. If you can change and adapt, you will flourish and shine. Those who stick to the old ways will struggle. Each paradigm shift forces leaders and teams to adapt to new ways, as follows:

1. Firms, teams and leaders can change faster than we ever thought before: *Be braver in how you lead and act.*
2. Remote working raises the bar for leaders, managers and team members: *Be more purposeful and deliberate in how you manage and work.*
3. Hybrid working is finally bringing leadership into the twenty-first century: *Acquire new skills for a new world of leadership.*

Here is what each of these challenges looks like in practice:

1 Be braver in how you lead and act
For 20 years, we had convinced ourselves that the pace of change was higher than ever in the twenty-first century. Then the pandemic arrived. Suddenly, we discovered what fast really looks like: the previous 20 years seem like a stroll in the park compared to the turbo-charged change caused by the pandemic. We discovered that leaders and teams are capable of far more extensive change, and far more rapidly, than anyone thought possible. Two examples will make the point:

- *The helpline for vulnerable people.* Managers of the charity Missing People always knew that, because of the sensitivity of the calls, the only way to ensure quality was to have the whole team working together in one place. That way, they could support each other, learn from each other and assure quality. Within 48 hours of lockdown, the service was being operated from team members' homes. They redesigned their technical infrastructure and operating systems so well that quality has gone up and they will never go back to the old way of working. The impossible became a better new normal within days.
- *Recruiting and training 1,700 teachers.* Teaching is an intense face-to-face activity. Trainee teachers need time in the classroom and time with experienced colleagues. Teach First, the UK's largest graduate recruiter, suddenly faced the challenge of having to recruit, select and train 1,700 teachers without being able to meet them in person. Within days, they had moved everything online and redesigned all their recruiting, selecting and training practices. They found some aspects of online working were more effective than when done face to

face. Coaches could spend more time with each trainee because they were not spending half the day travelling between schools. Online engagement with the training was very high. Teach First will now move to a hybrid online/offline approach to how they operate, which was unthinkable before the pandemic.

Missing People and Teach First are not alone in discovering that the pandemic has led to a new normal. Every organization has discovered that hybrid working is not a weak substitute for working in the office: it is better. Typically, firms have found that:

- Working from Home (WFH) is very good for 'thinking' work, such as reading and writing reports and presentations; it is surprisingly good for structured communications and collaboration, both one-to-one and at scale.
- The office is not dead. It is a wonderful machine for collaboration, building networks of trust and support, problem solving and creativity, spontaneous interactions, influencing people and decisions, mentoring new hires, building values, communicating quickly and managing easily.
- Mixing WFH and office work lets you achieve the best of both worlds, both in terms of productivity and mental health of staff.

The pandemic meant that all firms went through radical change at warp speed. Leaders discovered that they could achieve more

The office is not dead

change than they had ever dared to dream about, and they discovered that teams and staff can be far more agile and responsive than they had ever thought possible.

The pandemic forced change. It made leaders turn the impossible into reality. It has also turned managers into leaders. The only definition of leadership, which works well, comes from Henry Kissinger, the former US Secretary of State under Presidents Nixon and Ford:

'Leaders take people where they would not have got by themselves.'

That slightly dull definition is revolutionary. It suggests that there are plenty of people at the top of an organization who are not leading: they are simply administering a legacy they inherited. Meanwhile, there may be many people lower in the organization who are taking their teams where they would not have got by themselves: they may be managers by title but they are leaders by what they do. Leadership is not about your title: it is about what you do, regardless of what position you hold in your firm.

It has re-set expectations about how much change you should be able to achieve as a leader. The challenge for all leaders and managers is now clear: will you continue to be brave and bold or will you revert to the comfort zone of maintaining the new status quo? Managers can do exemplary work by managing the status quo and making incremental improvements: it is a much undervalued skill.

Leadership is not about your title: it is about what you do

But leaders should now ask themselves what other changes they should be making. The pandemic forced dramatic change, but what other unforced radical changes should your firm or team be making? What other 'impossible' changes should you now make? The best firms and best leaders will rise to this challenge and prosper.

If you know how you will take your team where it would not have got by itself, you will be leading. If you prefer to revert to the comfort zone of managing the new normal, you can still be a very good manager. However, the pandemic has raised the bar for leaders in term of how much change you can achieve. In Chapter 3 you will discover how you can maintain the pace of change and maintain your role as a leader.

2 Be more purposeful and deliberate in how you manage and work
Leading in the office is relatively easy: it is informal and ad hoc. You can see what is and is not working, and you can fix any problems in real time. Leading remotely you cannot afford to be informal and ad hoc. You have to be far more purposeful and deliberate in how you lead. This is very good news: it raises the bar for leaders. Leading remotely forces you to learn disciplines that make you a better leader in the office as well as outside it.

Managers cite six top challenges in moving from office to remote working:

- *Managing workloads and performance.* You can see who is struggling and who is coasting in the office. You have no idea if people are slacking or striving at home. In practice, many professionals strived too hard at home in an effort to prove their worth. That has led to mental health challenges, that many firms have found difficult to pick upon early or to manage remotely.
- *Communicating and co-ordinating.* The office is a wonderful machine for informal and intense communication. Everyone knows, more or less, what everyone else is doing. The water cooler and coffee machine enable spontaneous informal communication, learning and idea generation. It is hard to schedule spontaneity when you are working remotely.
- *Influencing people and decisions.* The people you need to influence are probably a few desks away in the office. If they are hard to reach, you can probably arrange to

'accidentally' bump into them at a meeting, at lunch or at the water cooler. Working remotely, you have to organize a call, which tends to turn an informal chat into a formal negotiation. It is easier to persuade as part of a casual chat than in a negotiation.

- *Resolving problems and misunderstandings.* If there is a problem or a misunderstanding in the office, it is easy to spot it and easy to fix it with a quick chat. If there is a problem or misunderstanding remotely, you can neither see it nor fix it until it is too late. The remote worker has time to ruminate on the misunderstanding and draw all the wrong conclusions.

- *Motivating is hard when managing remotely.* The first person to work out how to motivate by email will make a fortune, but it is a fortune that is unlikely to be made. As a manager, you have to create the conditions which enable your team to discover their intrinsic motivation. This is even harder when team members are isolated and lack the social support and routines provided by an office.

- *Setting goals* should be management 101, but turns out to be very hard when done remotely. In the office, goals can be discussed. As they are discussed, both understanding and buy-in tend to grow. The team understands not just the 'what' but also the 'why'; they understand the context, which allows them to make good judgement calls when necessary. Working remotely, it is easy to communicate the 'what', but it can be much harder to communicate the 'why' and the context. It is also hard to build buy-in without the informal dialogue of the office.

Faced with the extraordinary effects of the pandemic, firms have experimented to discover how to execute these core tasks remotely. It also revealed what works best in the office, and what works best remotely. However purposeful, deliberate and skilled a leader may be, there will always be some tasks which are best done in the office: creativity, innovation, mentoring, building trust and values are far easier in the office than over a video link.

The first person to work out how to motivate by email will make a fortune

3 Acquire new skills for a new world of leadership
The pandemic and the move to hybrid working have accelerated changes that have been underway for decades. The biggest change to leadership has little to do with technology and everything to do with the shift of power in the workplace. In the past, the boss had all the power. Unskilled workers in a one-factory town had nowhere else to go. But over time, the unskilled worker has morphed into the skilled professional who has plenty of career choices. Professionals can do more, but they also expect more; certainly, they expect a different sort of leadership. Most professionals do not like being micromanaged and probably think they can do your job better than you can.

WFH accelerates this power shift. In the office, the micromanager can still attempt to micromanage professionals. But WFH changes all that: you cannot see what your team is doing all the time and you cannot communicate with them all the time. WFH accelerates the move to far greater autonomy for team members, which in turn forces leaders to trust their team more. As a leader you have to be clear on the goals and trust your team on the process: let them use their skill to deliver for you. The more you trust them, the more likely they are to respond by rising to the challenge. The joy of employing professionals is that they all have pride and want to do a good job, and most of them want to over-deliver. By delegating more and trusting more, you also encourage your team to grow their skills and build their experience.

Not all leaders find it easy to let go. Some are resorting to intrusive surveillance software to maintain close control. This is a sure way to show you distrust your team and it is highly effective at destroying morale. In the short term it may give you the illusion of control. In the long term it makes it impossible to recruit top talent: the best professionals simply walk away from such management practices.

However, the power shift to greater autonomy, trust and delegation does have a dark side: greater accountability and stress. This is accentuated by hybrid working and WFH. In the office, your team can more easily know what they have to achieve because they can check with you and colleagues in real time. And they can also show they are working by being at their desk, or at least they can show they are present by leaving a jacket on their chair. But when they are working from home, there is no evidence that they are actually working. The only evidence is in the results they deliver.

Focusing on results is clearly desirable, but it can have unintended consequences. Occasionally, it can lead to less work: 'if I close a big sale on Monday morning, how much will I really feel I have to work for the rest of the week?' But more often it leads to overwork and stress.

Overwork comes from the ambiguous nature of office work. If you work in a factory, you can measure how many widgets you produced and you can measure the quality. Office work is harder to measure. If you have to produce a report, it could be one page or 100 pages long. However long it is, there will always be another fact you could gather or another opinion you could canvass. Effectively, you can never truly know when your work is complete.

WFH compounds the ambiguity of work. If professionals are inclined to over-achieve and over-deliver, they will continue working for as long as it takes to meet their own standards. WFH means that they have even greater incentive to over-deliver: they need to show that they were not shirking at home. And if they are worried about the job market, then over-delivery goes into overdrive. The result is long hours and stress: even when they stop working, people probably do not stop thinking about work. When work is in your home, it is very hard to switch off. COVID-19 is not just a physical health pandemic: it has also led to a quiet pandemic of mental health problems caused by work stress and social isolation.

In this new world, command and control skills have to be replaced by skills based on trust, persuasion and influence. You have to become the leader people want to follow, not the leader people have to follow because of the vagaries of the assignment system. This is good news. Influence allows you to exert far more power than your formal budget and span of control might imply. Chapter 1 shows you how you can build these future skills.

Become the leader people want to follow, not the leader people have to follow

Introduction and Summary – key points

1. The COVID-19 pandemic has forced the greatest shift in management and leadership in 200 years, for three reasons:
   - The discovery that firms and people are capable of faster and greater change than previously imagined possible.
   - Hybrid working forces leaders to become more purposeful and deliberate.

- Hybrid working forces the shift to twenty-first-century practices of more autonomy, trust, delegation and accountability.

2. Hybrid working is not a temporary shift, it is a permanent shift globally.

3. The office is not dead. It is a powerful machine for collaborating, communicating, building trust, and aligning goals and values.

4. WFH is very good for high-concentration solo work such as reading and writing reports, or coding, and works well with established teams.

5. WFH can lead to stress, ambiguity, isolation and loss of work-life balance. WFH is not for all: extroverts suffer, as do new and younger team members with challenging home-working conditions.

6. When done well, hybrid working leads to better work-life balance, more productivity and higher motivation.

7. Successful hybrid working is based on four principles:
   - Supportive relationships, not command and control.
   - More autonomy, which marches hand in hand with more accountability.
   - Motivation and mastery to sustain high performance.
   - Process: fix the plumbing of hybrid working.

8. Hybrid working only works where you have put in place the right plumbing:
   - Create the right rhythms and routines.
   - Provide the right technical, operational support.
   - Enable the team to discover what works best for them.

9. The pandemic has shown that firms, teams and people are far more agile and capable of change than previously imagined. Can we sustain the pace of change?

1

Relationships: build networks of trust and support to make things happen

The move to hybrid working has accelerated changes in how you can lead and manage. Hybrid working forces leaders to move from twentieth-century to twenty-first-century practices. In the office you can see who does what, which makes command and control easy. When teams work remotely, you have to trust that they do the right thing even when you cannot see them.

Traditional office management was based on high control and low trust. Now it is about high trust and less control. Command and control was very transactional; remote working depends on strong and supportive relationships. These are hard to build when working remotely.

In this chapter, you will discover:

- *The nature of the hybrid working revolution.*
- *How to become the trusted leader.*
- *How to build your network of influence.*

1.0 The nature of the hybrid working revolution

The hybrid working revolution is not just about learning to work from home (WFH). It is a revolution in leadership and management, and one that has been a long time in the making.

This particular revolution started with Machiavelli in the sixteenth century: he asked whether it is better for a leader to be feared or loved. He advised leaders to be feared, because love is fickle. For many years, this was how management worked. It was a command and control environment and the office was paradise for control-freak managers. In the office you can see who is doing what, and you can interfere at will. In the office, you don't need to rely on trust, because you can rely on control. Exercising close control is considerably harder when your team is far away: you can neither see nor hear them. You cannot be sure what they are doing: are they working, or walking the dog?

The office was paradise for control-freak managers

Command and control continued to work in the nineteenth century when workers had little education and few alternative sources of employment. As education levels have risen, workers have become professionals who can achieve more, but at the same time they expect more. The good news about professionals is that they have pride in their work and want to do well: with training, they do not need to be told how to do things. The bad news is that professionals may think that your job as a manager is irrelevant, and that they can do it better than you. They do not want to be micromanaged and are prepared to leave rather than put up with a boss they dislike: the number one reason for people leaving their employer is to leave their boss.

Twentieth-century management was about making things happen through the people you controlled. On the other hand, twenty-first-century management is about making things happen through people you do not control or do not want to be controlled. WFH means you can no longer micromanage your team. There are still some firms that use twenty-first-century technology to recreate nineteenth-century command and control: keyboard loggers,

WFH means you can no longer micromanage your team

location trackers and always-on video are signs of a firm deeply committed to command and control. These exceptions aside, it is clear that WFH means the days of command and control are over.

If you can no longer micromanage a team by observing them in the office, you have to trust them to perform. Trust is a two-way street: your team has to trust you to look after their interests. And this is the answer to Machiavelli's question: the true currency of leadership is neither fear nor love – it is trust.

You have to become the leader people *want* to follow, not the leader they are *told* to follow. You need to be respected by your team, your colleagues, your bosses and by all the stakeholders on whom you depend to succeed. This means you have to build your personal networks of trust and influence to make things happen through people you do not control – i.e., other departments and functions, and through customers, suppliers and partners. Trust and influence frees you from the confines of the command and control pyramid, and as a result you can make yourself as powerful as you want to be.

The task of the manager always has been, and always will be, to make things happen through other people. Hybrid working means you have to make the same things happen through other people whom you cannot see and cannot control directly. Trust and influence are your keys to success, but they are hard to acquire remotely. This chapter shows you how you can become the trusted leader who has influence far beyond your formal span of control. First, we need to understand what trust and influence actually mean.

Understanding trust

Trust is the glue that holds any team together. A true team is one where each team member cannot succeed without the support of other team members. Dependency is the hallmark of a team; if no one depends on anyone else, then you are just a group of individuals who happen to share the same boss.

Trust is the glue that holds any team together

Trust becomes more important when working remotely – as has been the case with the pandemic. You have to be able to trust that employees are doing the right thing even when you cannot see them. Trust is at the very heart of the hybrid working revolution.

Trust is the product of four variables, which you can develop:

- *Values alignment*. It is easier to work with people who are like ourselves: we understand them more easily because we may have shared experiences, shared culture and shared backgrounds. When we first meet someone from a completely different background, we may struggle to read their meaning and intentions. Values alignment is one reason many firms struggle with true diversity: we find it hard to trust people who are not like ourselves.
- *Goals alignment*. It is hard to trust someone who has a competing agenda that will undermine yours. But when you are all working to the same goal, trust comes more naturally: sports teams naturally foster trust because everyone is working towards the same goal, literally.

Within firms, there is as much competition as there is co-operation. It is an art form to align your interests with those of people in other parts of the business.

- *Credibility.* You probably have values alignment with your friends, which is why you chose them as your friends. But you might not choose to depend on them at work. To be credible you need the skills to do the job, and the track record that shows you do as you say. Credibility is like a vase: it takes time to build; it can be ruined in a moment of rashness and even if you can stick it together again, it is never quite the same. It is a precious commodity you have to nurture and protect.

- *Risk.* The greater the risk, the more trust you need. I might trust a stranger to tell me the way to the post office, but I would be unwise to trust the same person with my life savings. Smart managers learn to manage risk, often in unusual ways. Indeed, sometimes they manage risk by increasing it, not decreasing it.

Trust is essentially personal. You may trust the colleague to your left and distrust the colleague to your right. Each bond of trust has to be built up over time, which makes it a very valuable asset. It **Credibility is like a vase** also explains why it is often difficult to start work in a new firm: you simply do not have the networks of trust and influence that helped you to be effective in your previous role.

Understanding influence

Influence is how you extend your power beyond your formal area of control. Trust is personal; influence is your network of trusted relationships. Influence is the way you use your key asset of trust to make things happen. Your network of willing allies will keep you informed of developing events, advise you reliably when you need it, and help you influence decisions that affect your team and your future.

Influence is often confused with persuasion, but is fundamentally different. Persuasion is an event, a one-off transaction; influence is an enduring relationship.

Often, persuasion and influence pull in opposite directions. If I were a very clever, and amoral, salesman, I might persuade you to buy a second-hand car that promptly falls apart when you try driving it. If you next encounter me, after I have changed jobs to become a financial adviser, you will probably refuse to have anything to do with me: you will not trust me at all. Persuasion can destroy your network of influence.

To step up from trust to influence, managers need to master one more art: *enlightened selflessness*. You have to give in order to take, but if you always give then others will perceive you as being weak and they will take advantage.

The good news about influence is that it is self-reinforcing. Once you become influential, you attract more allies because of your apparent power to make things happen. More allies make you more powerful. Creating this virtuous circle takes time and is an investment that will pay off many times over.

The end of command and control?

It would be easy, although quite wrong, to claim that command and control has disappeared with the advent of remote working and new technology. In some conditions, technology has become an increasingly oppressive tool to control remote workers. Algorithms may help delivery drivers find the most efficient delivery route, but they also control the delivery driver closely. Such drivers have discovered that when your boss is an algorithm, your boss is a tyrant: it is always looking for more productivity; it is always monitoring you; it makes no effort to motivate you; and it is completely uninterested in your mental or physical health.

Even in the twenty-first-century world of hybrid working and flat organizations, the hierarchy reasserts itself at critical moments: performance assessment, pay and rewards, promotions and budget negotiations. Firms are becoming more equal, but some managers are more equal than others.

When your boss is an algorithm, your boss is a tyrant

The disciplines of management are harder to execute when managing a team of professionals you cannot see. Note the following seven examples:

- *Passing information up the hierarchy and passing orders down it* – but most information has been liberated by technology from the hierarchy. If knowledge is power, power is bypassing middle managers.
- *Monitoring progress and assuring quality* – this is much harder when you cannot see what team members are doing.
- *Assessing performance* – hybrid working forces greater autonomy and accountability for team members, making performance assessment more transparent.
- *Delegating work and assigning tasks* – delegating becomes harder because communicating is harder on a hybrid team. It is easy to communicate the 'what' needs to happen, much harder to convey the full context of 'why'.
- *Motivating and encouraging the team* – you cannot motivate a team by email or instant messaging.
- *Solving difficult challenges* – professionals do not want the most interesting challenges taken away from them. Hybrid working forces you not just to delegate more but to delegate more effectively.
- *Selecting, developing and progressing the team* – if they are not with the team in the office, new team members may

struggle to know who does what, build relationships and absorb the values of the team.

- *Securing budget and resources for the team* – it is harder to negotiate for budget and resources when you cannot work out the politics of budget time in the corridor and around the coffee machine in the office.

Each of these challenges of hybrid working will be explored in this book. Hybrid working forces managers to raise their game; you have to be more deliberate and purposeful in everything you do. Informal and ad hoc management worked well in the office: crises, mistakes, misunderstandings could all be solved in real time with the people in front of you. Managing in the office was forgiving of errors, because you could spot them and fix them fast. Managing a hybrid team, on the other hand, is unforgiving: miscommunications are hard to spot and may fester until it is too late.

In this chapter you will discover how to build the trust and influence you need for success in a hybrid team, and how to build a team that has strong trust:

- Build values alignment.
- Find goals alignment.
- Demonstrate credibility.
- Manage risk.
- Create your network of influence.

1.1 Build values alignment

The best hybrid teams have strong bonds of trust and strong common values. This means it is easier for well-established teams to work remotely than for new teams. It is hard for new team members to build the trusted relationships they need. The challenge of hybrid working is to sustain values alignment over time as the team evolves and changes. You can do this in four ways:

- Hire to values.
- Be a role model.
- Reinforce team values.
- Meet in person.

The test of values is not about what is written in the values statement. The real test of values is how people behave when they think no one is watching them. These are lived values you can rely on when team members are out of sight and working remotely.

1.1.1 Hire to values

Many bosses hire for skills and fire for values, or for a lack of the right values. This is a classic and natural mistake to make. If you see someone with all the right skills and experience for a hard-to-fill role, it is tempting to hire that person. But the right skills are no use if the individual is

> **Many bosses hire for skills and fire for values, or for a lack of the right values**

disruptive, manipulative, bullying or devious. Selecting to values is especially important on remote teams: new team members cannot absorb or adapt to the values of an office they cannot observe.

You can train new skills, but you cannot train new values. This means it is better to hire to values than to skills. An extreme version of this was developed by John Timpson, founder of a UK chain of shoe repair shops. These are small 'hole in the wall' sorts of shops, staffed by one or two people. It was, essentially, a massive exercise in remote working. He had to trust all his staff to do the right thing with every customer, every day. For years he made the mistake of hiring skilled cobblers, but found they did not provide the required customer service. So he started hiring to values and training people to become cobblers. To make sure that area managers hired to values, not skills, the interview form was a series of cartoon characters based on the Mr Men and Little Miss series. On one side of the form there were characters like Ms Helpful, Mr Honest, Ms Diligent, Mr Happy. On the other side the characters were Mr Lazy, Ms Grumpy, Mr Fib, Ms Messy. That simple sheet forced area managers to hire to values: they had no other choice. If you are really serious about hiring to values, then make sure your systems reflect that.

Every firm and team will have different values that matter to them. The firm-wide values statement is often of limited use, because it is a long list of platitudes designed to look good in the annual report and on a bronze plaque. If you are really serious about values, you will identify the three values most distinctive and important to the work of your team. No one will remember, let alone act on, 13 values. But they can remember three values, and you can focus like a laser on those values in recruiting and in reinforcing those values: over time, they become lived values.

A good way to think about values that matter is to think about how you want people to react when things go wrong. Three values stand out as being important for teams working remotely:

- Positive regard.
- Ownership.
- Kindness.

Positive regard is about believing that your colleagues are professionals who want to act in the best interests of the team. This value sounds innocuous, but is vital when working remotely. You will not be able to see that your colleagues are doing their best; you have to trust that they are doing so. Positive regard helps remote teams in at least three ways:

- When things go wrong. If you do not trust that colleagues are doing their best, you will quickly find yourself in the middle of a political blame game which goes nowhere fast. With positive regard, you will presume that there has been a misunderstanding and you will work collaboratively to solve it.
- Disagreements. A hallmark of effective teams is that they are prepared to disagree constructively, so that bad ideas are replaced with better ideas. Positive regard means that even when you attack an idea, you never attack a colleague. You earn respect by giving it, especially at awkward moments and in difficult conversations.
- Positive regard also helps in the good times. It encourages team members to appreciate and recognize each other's efforts. Positive regard becomes an effective form of peer group pressure which reinforces the right behaviours.

Ownership is a nice way of talking about accountability. On a remote team you cannot check that everyone is doing the right thing. You have to trust that they will take responsibility and do the right thing the right way. And you have to trust that, when things go wrong, they will find a solution. You cannot be with them all the time, sorting out

You earn respect by giving it

every problem they encounter. Teams that take ownership will perform better and learn faster than teams that escalate every problem up to the boss.

Kindness is not a feature of office life, but is important for remote working. If kindness sounds too touchy-feely, you can think of this as being *supportive*. Team members can feel isolated socially and struggle professionally with challenging and ambiguous workloads. Teams need to support each other both professionally and socially. You can bake in some of this support through the rhythms and routines you create for the team. Daily morning meetings enable the team to catch up professionally and identify where help is needed. You can create weekly social events for the team, and you can create Slack (or other communication) channels for gossip, hobbies and interests. But you also need team members who will support each other: you cannot do all the supporting yourself. Kind team members will reach out to each other for a chat; they will contribute to the banter and gossip on their Slack channels. Kind team members will also offer professional advice and support when needed, so that not all the problems of the team land upon your desk or screen.

1.1.2 Be a role model

If you want to discover the real values of a team watch the feet, not the mouth. In other words, actions speak far louder than words. If you wonder why your team is full of Machiavellian, back-stabbing politicians, look in the mirror. If your team is full of high performing, collaborative and enthusiastic team members, pat yourself on your back. Each team looks carefully at how their boss, and other bosses, behave. That is their guide to the lived values of the team.

The real test of values come at moments of truth. It is easy to display virtuous values while you are on easy street. But your team will really notice what you do when you are faced with difficult choices, difficult people and difficult situations. Crises are the perfect opportunity for you to

If you want to discover the real values of a team watch the feet, not the mouth

role model the behaviours you want in your team. Few people remember exactly who did what to whom and when in a crisis: too many things happen too fast. If no one remembers what you did, everyone remembers what you were like. Choose how you want to be remembered:

Role model A	Role Model B
Stressed	Calm
Blaming	Collaborating
Negative	Positive
Problem focused	Solution focused
Run around in circles	Move forwards

It is easy to default into type A, even if we think we are type B. Being the role model you want to be takes conscious effort, especially when it matters most.

The other moments of truth for you as a leader are promotion, bonus and assessment time. This is when you have to make hard choices. In any good team there are rarely enough promotions and bonuses to go round. You can never satisfy everyone. If you prioritize performance over behaviour everyone will understand what really matters. This is a classic challenge for many financial institutions: great performance and great behaviour do not always walk hand in hand. When the top performers get the top bonuses, in spite of their behaviour, then everyone understands what the real values are.

Choose how you want to be remembered

1.1.3 Reinforce team values

Throughout the year you will see people doing things the right way. Do not take this for granted. Catch people succeeding and celebrate it. After all, few people dislike praise from their boss. This is your chance to let each team member shine.

One mistake to avoid is criticizing the 'wrong' values and behaviours. Criticism itself can:

- *Be demoralizing:* no one likes being named and shamed, even in private.
- *Lead to arguments*: you will be asked to prove that the behaviour really was a breach of the values. This can be very hard to prove, unless it has been an exceptionally outrageous piece of conduct, which probably leads to disciplinary procedures anyway. But minor infractions are often a matter of interpretation. The argument normally concludes by both sides feeling aggrieved and misunderstood.
- *Be ineffective*: attacking values is the same as attacking people. They resist an attack on their identity and will not change. Instead, if you nurture the desired behaviours well enough, the new behaviours will – over time – simply drown out the old behaviours.

Again, John Timpson of shoe-repair shop fame is a good example of managing values remotely. He would drive around visiting all his shops and he kept a stash of small prizes in the back of his car. Whenever he found a good example of values in action, he awarded a prize on the spot. He had a goal of making sure he praised at least 10 times as often as he criticized. In practice, he then found that the one time in 10 could always be reframed as positive support and coaching. If you want to change behaviour, praise is always going to be more powerful than criticism.

Catch people succeeding and celebrate it

Although boss praise is good, peer praise is better, so put positive peer group pressure to work. And while peer pressure is good, peer praise is even better. Encourage your team to give positive feedback to each other, both for work and for values.

Peer praise is particularly well suited to remote working. The joy of platforms such as Slack is that they are shared platforms so everyone can see the praise. The practice of praise creates a virtuous circle:

- The praised person feels good for being praised in public.
- The person giving the praise feels good, not least because they often receive praise themselves for giving praise.
- The praised person will often reciprocate the praise.
- All team members see the value of giving and receiving praise, and so are more likely to join in.

In a world in thrall to social media, there are obvious opportunities to gamify this system of praise. The hunt for 'likes' on social media is in danger of turning us all into dopamine junkies: we are hooked on social media in search of the next 'like' and the next little hit of dopamine. By gamifying the praise system, people with the most 'likes' or 'praises' from their peers might win a small prize. If the prizes are large, however, the gamification ceases to be collaborative fun: it becomes a competition to win and can undermine the teamwork you want to foster. Similarly, gamification of praise only works in the right culture. In more traditional firms, gamification will be seen as a contest to win, which will then be reflected in any year-end assessments. This leads to dysfunctional behaviour, as team members will be fighting each other to prove who the best team player is.

1.1.4 Meet in person

All the research on remote and global teams leads to one essential conclusion: at some point, you have to meet in person. This is the single most important thing you can do to make the team work well. When the team meets in person, everyone gets to know each other; you build values alignment and trust, which will help you throughout the rest of the year.

Even teams that work 100 per cent remotely feel the need to gather as a team at least once a year. The business purpose of the meetings will involve a mix of training, planning, reviewing and workshops. The danger is that the organizers feel obliged to fill the schedule with business matters to justify the cost and expense of flying people around the world to meet each other. This can be a mistake. Social bonding is just as important as business matters. Once people know each other, trust increases and the quality of communication improves dramatically.

Leave plenty of time in the agenda for socializing. As part of that, you may need to encourage people to move out of their normal bubble. A common sight at conferences is that people who share the same geography, function or seniority all socialize together: they socialize with people they already know and trust. This is human nature: we prefer the comfort of our own support bubble and we are happy to live in an echo chamber where we hear views like our own. This is also a missed opportunity: a team gathering is a chance for everyone to get to know each other. Making this happen effectively requires some careful planning: you want to make sure that people who need to meet are able to find each other. Small group activities and meal seating plans are perfect opportunities to organize some carefully choreographed business dates.

At some point, you have to meet in person

1.2 Find goals alignment

Achieving goals alignment represents two challenges:

- *Vertical challenge*: gaining commitment, not just compliance, from your direct reports.

- *Horizontal challenge*: gaining the support of other departments, stakeholders, customers or suppliers who will have different priorities and agendas from you: why should they help you?

1.2.1 The vertical challenge

In the days of command and control, achieving goals alignment was easy: orders came from the top and everyone was expected to do as they were told. Unsurprisingly, this no longer works. Professionals do not like being bossed around. If you order them to do something, at best you will achieve compliance but not commitment; at worst, your orders will be challenged if your team thinks they make no sense. If you want to make things happen, you need more than grudging compliance – you need commitment. You need committed professionals who will identify problems, find solutions, deal with opposition and roadblocks, and react well to the unexpected. If you have no more than compliance, you will find that all these challenges and problems will be escalated back up to you and you will have an impossible job on your hands. You need professionals who can deal with a volatile, uncertain, complex and ambiguous world on your behalf. That means you need goals alignment, which in turn gains their full commitment.

In the office, the alignment process happens informally through endless formal and informal conversations with different stakeholders. Alignment does not come from revealing **Professionals do not like being bossed around** the goal in an email or a PowerPoint presentation. Such online messages communicate what needs to happen, but may fail to convey the vital context or answer 'why' the goal matters. Alignment comes from a process of discovery in which each person works out the context and the 'why' from their own perspective:

- Why does this matter to me?
- What is my role in this?
- How does this fit with my other priorities?
- How important is it for my appraisal?
- What is the minimum acceptable outcome and what does 'great' look like?
- What are the main risks and obstacles, and how can we deal with them?
- How do the practicalities work: what is needed by when for whom, what support do I need and are there any interim checkpoints?

The answers for these questions will be different for each person, because each person has a different role to play. Until they discover the answers to these questions, it is hard for them to be truly committed to your goal. If the task is simple, the context can be discovered in a five-minute conversation. If it is a more challenging, complex goal, it may take a series of discussions for your team member truly to understand and commit to what is expected. When people discover a solution, they own it; when it is revealed to them in a memo, they neither own it nor are committed to it. The discovered answer is more powerful than the revealed answer, although it takes more time and effort on both sides to discover the answer.

The discovered answer is more powerful than the revealed answer

This process of discovery is ad hoc, informal and repetitive. It is precisely the sort of conversation that is well suited to the office and poorly suited to remote working. The obvious solution is to make sure you have goal-setting conversations in the office, which enables the process of discovery and alignment to happen. Working remotely, you can still set simple goals (although see Chapter 2 on delegation for more details). For more ambitious and complex goals, you need to be more purposeful and deliberate in how you re-create the discovery process. The minimum you should expect is:

- *Pre-brief.* This is a short conversation in which you outline the goal, indicating what you need from your team members to get there. Set the expectation of a full briefing to follow. This gives your team members time to think about all the questions they would like to ask, and suggestions they would like to make.
- *Full briefing.* This is your chance to lay out the full context as you understand it and to answer or explore any questions and suggestions. Quantity and quality of questions shows that your team members are engaged and starting to own the goal.
- *Follow up.* Expect at least one follow up: any answers in the briefing may well give rise to more questions. Unanswered questions lead to confusion and anxiety, which help no one.
- *Regular check-ins.* A good remote team discipline is to start each day with a morning call (see Chapter 4 for details). These ensure that if your team members need help, you can give it promptly.

A common mistake is to attempt to 'sell' the goal. Even CEOs make this mistake when they make a grand and impressive presentation about new corporate objectives. It is a mistake because the more you sell, the more the goal is seen as your goal, not theirs. Instead, use the discovery process to transfer ownership of the goal from you to your team.

1.2.2 The horizontal challenge

Managers today have to make things happen through people they do not control. You need the support of people outside your team, and possibly outside your firm, to succeed. The problem is that they have different priorities from you. These priorities may conflict or compete with your needs, so why should they help you?

Managers today make things happen through the people they do not control

If you want to persuade anyone to do anything, you can use four forms of communication, in descending order of effectiveness.

- *In-person.* A private face-to-face conversation is the best way to broker a deal. You can understand their needs and limitations and find a way through which works for you both. In private, both of you will be more flexible and reasonable than in public. Once someone takes a position in public (a third person makes any meeting public), they find it very hard to reverse their position.
- *Face-to-face by video.* This works reasonably well where you already have an established relationship of trust. The less trust you have managed to establish, the harder this sort of conversation becomes. It turns from a problem-solving discussion into a negotiation that may not be a win-win.
- *Person-to-person by phone.* Phone works less well than video because you are unable to read and interpret any reactions.
- *Asynchronous communication:* email, messaging, snail mail. This gives the other person time to think, but gives you no chance to engage in a problem-solving dialogue where you can reach a mutually acceptable

outcome. Few people are persuaded or motivated by an email, unless it is a very simple transaction such as arranging the time for a call.

As with the vertical challenge, persuading colleagues is done best in the office. Often the conversation is simple. If you have an established basis of trust, then most colleagues will be willing to help, even if only because of two self-interested reasons:

- Helping you is less hassle and less risky than not helping you and gaining a poor reputation in the office. The office grapevine can be fast and merciless when it comes to reputations. Working remotely, behaviour is hard to observe so there is less risk in being unhelpful.
- Helping you sets up the expectation that you will return the favour in some way in future.

The art of persuasion, remotely or in person, is a whole other book. In practice, persuasion is about risk and reward. If you are persuading remotely, you have to apply this risk-reward principle carefully and deliberately.

- *Reward* is about the WIFM factor: What's In It For Me? If you can find a win for the other person in helping you, then you are on the path to success. A win might be something very simple: 'I will look good in front of my boss; I will get support from you for my agenda; I will be able to get one more distraction off my to-do list.'
- *Risk* is about the risk to your colleague of helping you. Risk is not logical, it is personal and emotional: 'Will this take my time; will I be seen to look stupid supporting this idea; will I open the floodgates to lots of other demands for help?' The obvious solution is that you should reduce the risk of action. The less obvious

solution is that you should increase the risk of inaction. At its simplest, this comes in the form of the unsubtle threat: 'The CEO wants this tomorrow...' Slightly subtler is to use peer group pressure: 'Everyone else is behind this, I hope you can help as well...' No one wants to stand alone in stopping something happening.

The joy of hybrid working is that it allows you to work on the right things in the right places. Achieving goal alignment is

Risk is not logical, it is personal and emotional

suited to office work, so do it there if you can. If you have to do it remotely, take the opportunity to practise your persuasion skills and remember the key points:

- Two ears and one mouth: listen more than you talk.
- The discovered solution is valued more than the revealed solution: don't sell, discuss the goal.

1.3 Demonstrate credibility

Credibility is about doing as you say. No one will trust a colleague who does not do as they say.

All professionals like to believe that they do as they say. Curiously, most professionals do not believe that their colleagues always do as they say: there is a yawning gap between how we see ourselves and how we see others. There is a reason for this gap: we judge ourselves by our intentions and we judge others by their actions. We know that we always do our best with the best of intentions. Unfortunately for us, colleagues cannot observe our intentions – they can only see our actions, so that is what they judge us on.

The credibility challenge is not in the doing, it is in the saying. You can rely on professionals when it comes to doing: they will usually do their best and they usually have high standards and high expectations of themselves. This can lead to perfectionism and professional burnout.

'Saying' is at the heart of the credibility problem. In the office you have constant opportunities to adjust expectations. You pick up quickly if there has been a misunderstanding and you can react in real time. Working remotely, you have to be far more careful in what you say. Careless talk costs credibility. There are three mistakes professionals make when it comes to 'saying':

We judge ourselves by our intentions and we judge others by their actions

- Failing to say 'no'.
- Failing to set yourself up for success.
- Accidentally over-committing.

Building credibility is not just about what you do and say, it is also about how you are. We should not judge a book by its cover, and we should not judge people by how they look. But we do. So the fourth element of building credibility is:

- Acting the part.

1.3.1 Failing to say 'no'

Professionals strive to please and are willing to take on challenges as a test of their abilities. This leads them to agree to take on commitments which perhaps they should not take on. We have all been in that position from time to time, when we leave a meeting and then think to ourselves 'why on earth did I agree to do that?' What follows are long nights and endless stress in the attempt to deliver on an unwise commitment. Even if you then heroically deliver the essential 90 per cent of what was expected, you will still have lost all credibility. You will be judged not by your noble intentions but by your practical actions, which fell short of expectations.

Saying 'no' to your boss can be as career limiting as saying 'yes' and taking on an impossible challenge. In many firms, staff know that 'no' is a no-no. You need a creative way of saying 'no' while appearing to say 'yes'. The creative alternative is to have a discussion about how you can set the assignment up for success. That is a positive discussion which bosses embrace. If the goal is genuinely impossible, then the 'success' discussion will help your boss discover this for themselves.

Many people find it easier to say no when they are meeting remotely, simply because there is less emotional engagement and pressure. It is easier to be rational and logical on video because you have more distance, and you know that when the conversation finishes you no longer have to look the boss in the face. If you are a boss, make sure discussions about challenges happen face-to-face in the office, where you are much less likely to hear 'no' as an answer.

In many firms, staff know that 'no' is a no-no

1.3.2 Failing to set yourself up for success

A challenging assignment is a chance to prove yourself, but it is also a chance to fail. You have to set yourself up for success. Just as most battles are won and lost before the first shot is fired, so most projects succeed or fail before they start. It does not matter how heroic you are, if the set up is wrong you will not succeed. Heroic failures are not heroic, they are simply failures.

Setting yourself up for success means that you need to have the right expectations and resources to achieve the ends. You have to discuss:

- Budget.
- Timescales.

- Staffing.
- Priorities.
- Preferred approach to the challenge.
- Potential obstacles and how they will be dealt with.
- Support and approvals required.
- Who else needs to be involved and why.
- Milestones and check-in points.
- What 'good' looks like at the end.

Many professionals find this is a difficult conversation because it sounds demanding. It should not be difficult: it is a credibility-enhancing discussion. 'Setting up success' is a discussion most bosses want. By working through all the detail, you demonstrate that you have understood the scale and scope

Most projects succeed or fail before they start

of the challenge and that you are taking full ownership of it. That is a very positive sign for the boss.

Do not be afraid of asking for what is required. When I decided to start a bank, I worked out that I needed an initial £1 billion of capital. When I asked for this sum, the reaction was: 'If you had asked for any less you would not have been serious'. When you show you understand what it really takes, you enhance your credibility and you enhance your chances of success.

This discussion works well on video, provided that you already have a good level of trust with the boss and the issue is not huge. But if you are asking for £1 billion from a funder to start a bank, that is a high-risk conversation which has to be undertaken in person. The higher the risk, the more trust you need to build, and trust is always easier to build in person than remotely.

1.3.3 Accidentally over-committing

This is one of the most common causes of arguments and loss of credibility. Imagine a colleague or team member comes to you with a slightly awkward request. Out of courtesy, you do not refuse to help. Being a good team member or boss, you decide to give a helping hand. So you tell your colleague something like:

- 'OK – I will see what I can do'.
- 'I will do my best'.
- 'I will look into it'.

Being diligent, you do your best. You look into it and you discover that the request cannot be fulfilled. So you go back to your colleague, and give the bad news. You may hope to be thanked for showing goodwill. Instead, you suddenly find that you have lost all credibility with your colleague. What went wrong?

You know that you were not agreeing to your colleague's request. But what was said and what was heard were completely different. You were giving yourself lots of escape clauses for not delivering. But what was heard was not 'I will do my best' but 'I will do it'. At this point, you may find yourself in the 'I said, you said, she said, but he didn't and they should have, if you could have' discussion. It is a discussion in which both sides convince themselves they are right and that they are the injured party. This is an impossible discussion because there is no good outcome to it.

It is better to have a difficult conversation about expectations before you start, than to have an impossible conversation about outcomes when you finish. Be crystal clear about the expectations you are agreeing to. Curiously, this is a conversation that is easier to have remotely. In the office, it is too easy to make a casual commitment in a short conversation in the corridor. The commitment happens without really thinking about it. When you are remote, there is more distance and more formality. You have more time to think about what is being discussed, because you are not rushing to the next meeting.

Whether online or in person, try to maintain constant guard against making unintended commitments.

1.3.4 Acting the part

Some of the least trusted professions dress the most conservatively. Politicians, estate agents and bankers have been among the last holdouts for the suit and tie, but they also rank near the bottom of the IPSOS-MORI veracity survey, which assesses public trust in different professions. The suit and tie is an attempt to redress the trust gap which these professions have. The more serious the occasion, the more likely you are to see a politician dressing in a suit and tie. Similarly, the more important the business occasion, the more likely people are to dress smartly and formally. Ripped jeans, old sneakers and unkempt hair probably is not the best start to a job interview, on either side of the table.

If you want to be credible, you have to look and act the part. There is no universal rulebook for how you should look or act. The basic principle is that credibility is in the eye of the beholder: dress and act in such a way that others perceive you positively. If you want to be credible with your mates on a Friday evening, you will dress and act one way; if you want to be credible with the boss of your boss, you will dress and act differently. This is where you have to learn the norms of your firm and your function. In some firms, wearing a tie would mark you out as strange; in other settings, it may still be expected.

In the office, the pressure to conform is high. Being in constant contact with your colleagues shows you what normal dress and behaviour looks like, and peer group pressure makes conformity desirable. Make sure that you conform to the right

If you want to be credible, you have to look and act the part

role model; what looks right in the post room may not look right in the boardroom. If you want to be seen as someone who belongs at a more senior level, see how more senior people dress. Every firm, every function, every level has its own unwritten dress code which varies by type of occasion. Decipher the code in order to prosper.

Working online means it is not so clear what the norms of behaviour are. Out of the office, there is not the constant pressure to conform to how your colleagues act and dress. It is easy to let dress standards slip. Doing video calls in pyjamas may be possible, but not advisable. A simple way to maintain boundaries between home and work when you are WFH (working from home) is to change clothes: have different work and leisure clothes even at home. This allows you to switch off mentally at the end of the day, and then stay focused in working hours.

1.4 Manage risk

More risk requires more trust:

- Would you trust a stranger in the street to give you directions to the post office?
- Would you trust a stranger in the street with your life savings?

The same principle applies at work. You might trust a new team member with a simple task to start with, but you are unlikely to entrust your most important project to someone who is untried, untested and unproven. Working on any team involves risk: you have to take risk because on any team you depend on other team members to achieve your collective goals. The more trust you have, the more risk you are prepared to share. This means that well-established teams have been able to continue reasonably well with WFH: new teams and new team members may struggle because they have not established the bonds of trust that enable the team to operate effectively.

This means that normally you have to manage risk either by increasing trust (so that you can take more risk) or by reducing risk, which can be both rational and emotional. But there is another way of managing risk well: by increasing risk. All risk is relative, and if you increase the perceived risk of doing nothing, that is a good way of encouraging people to do something which they might otherwise see as being risky. In this section we will look at:

- Reducing rational risk.
- Reducing emotional risk.
- Increasing risk.

1.4.1 Reducing rational risk

Rational risk is relatively easy to deal with. Most firms understand how to manage this sort of risk. A staple item for board or Finance Committee meetings is the risk review. The risk register will rank all the risks for severity and likelihood, and will have a note about the mitigating actions to be taken. Firms also work hard to mitigate customers' perceptions of risk. Product guarantees are a simple way of reducing perceived risk; buyer reviewers on websites can help, assuming they have not been gamed; and certificates on your doctor's wall assure you that he or she is not a quack who will accidentally kill you.

Within the firm, you have many ways of reducing the logical risk of any new idea:

- Conduct further research.
- Do a market/product test.
- Phase implementation and funding.
- Bring in experts to deliver or advise.

These rational discussions happen as easily online as they do in person. The discussion may be testing and exhausting, but they are essentially simple and straightforward; people, teams and firms are normally good at finding rational solutions to known problems.

1.4.2 Reducing emotional risk

What is emotional about the decision to buy a photocopier? It appears to be the ultimate rational decision which will involve trade-offs between speed, quality and cost per page. Simple. But now imagine the scene where the CEO needs a hard copy of the speech she is about to give in 15 minutes, and the photocopier breaks down. Do you want to be the office idiot who let the CEO down by buying an unreliable photocopier? Even the simplest rational decision has an emotional element to it. Emotional risk asks 'how will this decision affect me personally?'

- Will this require more work by me?
- Will I look like an idiot if it goes wrong?
- Will I get any recognition if it goes right?
- How will this affect my performance appraisal?
- Will this help me hit my year-end goals, or is it a distraction?
- Will I be alone in supporting/opposing this?

It is natural to have these thoughts when presented with a new idea. It is also natural not to express them directly, because they appear selfish and unprofessional concerns. Instead, emotional objections are often expressed as rational objections. This causes grief. If you tackle the rational objection, you may find more rational objections crop up while the real objection remains hidden.

Even the simplest rational decision has an emotional element to it

The discussion becomes a dispute which goes round in circles. Fighting emotion with reason is like fighting fire with gas. It is best enjoyed as a spectator sport, not as a participant.

This is your chance to deploy the tea bag theory of leadership: there is no problem that cannot be solved over a cup of tea. The best way to discover and deal with emotional risk is a cup of tea, in private and in person. This is your chance not to challenge, but to listen. If you listen long enough people often talk themselves into submission. This is hard to do on a video call, and impossible if other people are present. You can deal with reason and logic when WFH. You cannot deal with emotion and politics remotely, unless you have already established a very high level of trust and can talk about personal feelings and perspectives by video.

1.4.3 Increasing risk

Would you like to spend the night on a raft in the middle of the Atlantic surrounded by icebergs? Unless you are an adventurer, this is the sort of invitation you are likely to decline. But many people on the ill-fated *Titanic* were fighting each other to take up exactly such an invitation. First class passengers, used to a life of luxury, were the first to get into the life rafts. Spending a night on a life raft was a far less risky option than going down with the *Titanic*. All risk is relative. If you can show that the risk of doing nothing is greater than the risk of doing something, people will happily follow your risky course of action.

Fighting emotion with reason is like fighting fire with gas

CEOs often increase perceived risk when they want to sell an unpopular course of action, such as a major restructuring. They will take great pains to show that disaster will follow if the restructuring does not happen: a little pain now to avoid great pain later. The CEO selling the restructuring is working rational risk, and you can do the same when you want to push a difficult agenda. But you can also increase the emotional and political risk of doing nothing. Peer group pressure is highly effective: no one wants to be the one person stopping something from happening. Find some early allies for your idea and build a bandwagon effect: most colleagues will find it easier to go along with the bandwagon than to try to stop it.

These sorts of risk discussions are delicate and require more listening than talking: you need to find out what colleagues really think, hope and fear. You cannot do that by talking all the time. These are office sorts of conversations: know what conversations are best suited to where. Rational and transactional discussions work well remotely. Personal and political discussions are best face to face, in private and in the office.

All risk is relative

1.5 Create your network of influence

Influence is the informal power you wield to influence people and decisions you do not control. It is the way you make the firm you work for, work for you. In Japan they talk about 'reading the air'. In other words, you have to know who, where, when and how you can push. You need to know when to step up and when to step back. If this sounds political to you, you are right. In practice, the more senior you become, the more you need to master the arts of influence and politics. This is hard enough in the office, where you can 'read the air': you meet people in the corridor, outside meeting rooms and at the water cooler. You can find out who is thinking and planning what, and you can influence people with informal and ad hoc chats. None of this is possible with remote working. In theory, remote working should lead to more formal and objective management with less politics. In the meantime, we have to deal with reality.

The starting point for building influence is to build your own network of trust and support. Your network is self-reinforcing: the stronger it is, the stronger it becomes. The hallmark of an influential manager is that they know what is going on and are able to make things happen. This means colleagues are likely to turn to them when they need help, when they have ideas, and when they hear rumours or have information. Less influential colleagues have less access to the information flow and less ability to make things happen.

We have already explored how you can build trust in the office, and how it is harder to build remotely. Here are four principles for building your influence in a hybrid workplace:

- Step up at moments of truth.
- Build your claim to fame.
- Give to take.
- Go where the power is.

You may find that it is far easier to build influence if you are in the office than when you work remotely. In the office, unsurprisingly, you will have greater access to information, colleagues and decision makers than when you work remotely. If you can, it still pays to be in the office to stay in the flow and build your career: if you want a job, work remotely; if you want a career, go to the office.

1.5.1 Step up at moments of truth

In any firm there are moments of uncertainty, ambiguity and crisis when no one is sure what to do. These are the moments you can see power visibly ebb and flow across a conference room table. Some people have the courage to step up, others step back to avoid risk and effort. The simple act of suggesting a solution is both

If you want a job, work remotely; if you want a career, go to the office

constructive and powerful: you may well be asked to step up and implement your idea.

In practice, these moments of truth are rarely unexpected. Normally, you will have a good sense that a problem, challenge or opportunity is brewing if you keep yourself informed. You can then decide if this is your moment to step up or step back, and you can plan accordingly. Your apparently spontaneous idea or solution should in fact be well planned. Unplanned spontaneity can lead to accidents and unwise commitments.

Working remotely, you are working blind. You are not in the information flow: you can neither see nor evaluate the opportunities or crises emerging, and you have no idea if other people are stepping up and competing with you or not. If you have to work remotely, make extra effort to stay in the information flow. Slack channels may have some relevant gossip, but you also need to find out what is *not* in the public domain. Find the opportunity to talk with colleagues around the firm: you can normally find an excuse to call people in HR, planning or finance who may well know more about what is going on and what is being planned. Be helpful to them and they will help you. Office politics and gossip does not stop when you leave the office. Make sure you stay informed: you need to know what *will* happen, not just what *has* happened.

1.5.2 Build your claim to fame

Careers are built on claims to fame. In the movies, actors toil for years before they have a breakthrough performance: this is their claim to fame that launches their career. In business, most leaders have some claim to fame that has acted as their career catapult:

Know what will happen, not just what has happened

it might be that they launched a new product, turned around an ailing business or acquired a big new client. But it could also be that they become known for their expertise in one area: one colleague of mine became a world expert at developing business cases for large ($50 million plus) systems integration projects in the life insurance industry. It was an arcane skill, which kept him in high demand. Unfortunately, it was a job he hated, so make sure your claim to fame gives you the career you want.

A good claim to fame is one that has visibility and relevance across the firm. This means it will stretch you, but at the same time it will ensure you are noticed. As with moments of truth, you need to be in the information flow to know which opportunities are the right ones for you. You also need to set yourself up for success. If you take on a **Careers are built on claims to fame** challenge without doing this, you will not have a claim to fame: it's likely you will fail and instead have a claim to infamy.

1.5.3 Give to take

It is not enough to have a claim to fame: you have to stake your claim. If failure is lonely, then success is a very crowded space. You will suddenly find that everyone who offered you five minutes of mediocre advice is claiming that they were at the heart of your success. So how do you deal with all this competition for the credit?

Do not try to compete with all the people claiming success. You will simply become another voice in the cacophony of competing claims. Instead, do something counter-intuitive: give all your credit away to everyone else. When a colleague claims credit for giving you advice, even if it was useless, lavish her with praise for the wonderful insight she gave. This does two very powerful things for you:

- You show that you were the leader of the effort: the leader is the only person who is in the position to know who did what.

- You win friends and allies. Competing with them for credit makes them competitors; giving them credit makes them allies who might even be grateful for the recognition you secure for them.

The 'give to take' principle is not just about your claim to fame. It is a broader principle about praise. How many people think that they are over-recognized, over-praised and overpaid? In a world where people are starved of praise, you will find that 'thank you' is powerful, simple and underused. So use it more. And even more powerful is praise that reaches the ears of their boss or colleagues. The person you praise will not only feel the need to reciprocate, but will also believe that you have very fine judgement to recognize excellence which no one else could see.

Give to take also applies to helping your colleagues. Be generous with your time and you build up a credit of goodwill with colleagues. But do not be completely selfless. If you help out and get nothing in return, you are being exploited. Help should be reciprocal: the 'tit for tat' principle again applies.

1.5.4 Go where the power is

Willie Sutton, the famous bank robber, was asked why he robbed banks. 'Because that is where the money is', came the apocryphal reply. If you want fame, go where the fame is. If you want power, go where the power is.

How many people think they are over-praised and overpaid?

Working for the right boss on the right project can be a ticket to the Promised Land; working for the wrong boss and on the wrong project is more likely to be a one-way ticket to the wilderness. Assignment time is when you discover that career is both a noun and a verb. If you manage your career well, career is a noun where you steadily progress with the right bosses and assignments to the right roles. If you do not manage this well, you will find that your career becomes a verb: you will career wildly from one unexpected episode to another, from triumph to disaster and back again (hopefully). Careering can be fun, but a career can be more rewarding.

You only excel at what you enjoy

The 'right' assignment is a subjective assessment where you have to ask yourself four questions. These questions are easy to ask, but often hard to answer:

- Is it set up for success: can I succeed? Be prepared to have difficult conversations before you start about goals, expectations, resources and budget. Your negotiating strength goes from high to zero the moment you say 'yes' to a new role or project.
- Does it have visibility across the firm? You need a claim to fame, and you need to be noticed. Countless colleagues do well, but you have to find a way of shining even more brightly than they do.
- Will I learn skills which will help me in future? A good role will stretch you. If it does not stretch you, you are probably going nowhere fast. A key test is whether you will be learning explicit and tacit skills which will help you build your career.
- Will I enjoy it? You only excel at what you enjoy. Excellence and success takes huge effort, which you can sustain only if you enjoy it. And life is too short to do things you hate for bosses you dislike: that is a recipe for failure and misery.

1.6 Key points

1. Trust and respect is the currency of leadership: informal power lets you achieve more than formal command and control alone.
   - Trust is the glue that holds teams together. Teams are based on mutual dependency; where there is no dependency, there is no team. Remote working requires more trust than when you can see your team in person.
   - Meet in person to build trust. Trust is easier to build in person than remotely.
2. Align values across your team.
   - Select to values, not just to skills.
   - Be a role model and live the values you want your team to show.
   - Reward and recognize behaviours which show the right values in action.
3. Align goals with your team members.
   - Ensure they understand the context of the goal: the 'why' as well as the 'what'.
   - Let the team discuss and discover what the goal really means for them: the discovered truth is valued more than the dictated truth.
4. Align goals with other stakeholders across the firm. Listen to persuade: use your two ears and one mouth in that proportion.
5. Build your credibility: do as you say.
   - Saying, not doing, is the biggest problem: unwise and unintended commitments.
   - Set yourself up for success: have difficult conversations before you start.
   - Be ready to say 'no' and do not over-commit.
   - Act the part: we are still judged on how we look and act.

6. Manage risk: emotional and political risk is more dangerous than rational risk.
   • You can manage risk by reducing the risk of action, or increasing the perceived risk of inaction.
7. Build your network of influence to make the firm work for you. This is easier in the office than remotely. If you want a job, work remotely; if you want a career, go to the office.
   • Step up at moments of truth.
   • Build your claim to fame.
   • Give to take.
   • Go where the power is.

2

Autonomy and accountability to drive action

The pandemic has accelerated the leadership revolution, and autonomy and accountability is at the heart of the revolution. WFH leads to higher autonomy because you have to trust your team to do the right thing when you can neither see nor hear them in person. Remote teams can sustain the status quo well. However, the real challenge for any team and any leader is whether you can drive change, even when the team is remote. The new world of autonomy and accountability leads to three challenges for leaders and managers, which this chapter will address:

- *Managing professionals remotely: managing better by managing less.*
- *Recrafting your role as a leader in a world of high autonomy.*
- *Driving change and sustaining the revolution.*

2.0 The autonomy and accountability challenge

Professionals today expect far more autonomy than the armies of semi-educated workers who powered the Industrial Revolution. Many managers have found this hard to deal with, because the old ways of command and control have been deeply ingrained in management for over 200 years. Managers have lost their coercive power in the face of skilled staff. The more skilled staff become, the more they are able to find work elsewhere if they do not like the way you manage; the number one reason for people leaving a job is to leave a boss they dislike. Today, you have to become the manager people want to work for, not the manager people have to work for as a result of the assignment system.

The pandemic accelerated this revolution because it is much harder to control people when you cannot see them. WFH eliminates your ability to hear, see and sense what your team is doing. You have to trust that they are working well and behaving well when they are out of sight. WFH and hybrid working is forcing managers to find new ways of managing in a world of high autonomy and low direct control.

Autonomy and accountability is also a challenge for team members. The joy of increased autonomy is balanced by the terror of increased accountability: you cannot have one without the other. Remote and hybrid working increases both autonomy and accountability for team members. Done well, this can be an undisguised blessing; done poorly, it is a recipe for anxiety, stress and overwork. This chapter focuses on how your role as a leader changes as a result of the revolution. (Chapter 3 shows how team members can thrive in this revolution.)

2.1 Managing professionals remotely: managing better by managing less

How do you manage people who don't like to be managed and who you can neither see nor hear for most of the time? The answer is simple: manage less, lead more.

Working in an office encourages management, not leadership. When you can see and hear your team all day, it is natural to believe that you add value by managing them. The classic tasks of management included assigning work, managing performance, checking quality, dealing with crises and conflicts, sorting out the most challenging problems and helping the team develop. In other words, the job of the manager was to interfere with the team's work. This was necessary when the team had fewer skills: they needed direction and checking; they needed someone to sort out problems, crises and conflicts for them. But these activities no longer add value when the team is highly skilled and highly motivated.

WFH makes close supervision, the hallmark of office management, impossible. You cannot see and hear your team all day when they are at home. You are forced to trust them more. As we have seen, trust is the essence of any team. If no one on the team depends on anyone else you do not have a team: you have a group of individuals working to their own goals. Teamwork is about dependency, and that means you have to be able to trust your team.

The trust challenge for you as a team leader is delegation. The more you are prepared to delegate, the more you trust your team. The less you delegate and the more you check your team, **Manage less, lead more** the less you trust your team. Team leaders often find very good excuses for not delegating. Below are the normal excuses and what the team hears, in brackets:

- I can do it better myself (I don't trust my team's ability).
- This report is vital and I am accountable for it (I am not dumb enough to trust my team on anything that actually matters).
- I don't have time to train the team for this (I don't trust them to do this, and I do not want my team to upstage me).
- My boss asked me for this personally (I don't trust my team and I want to stay in control).

- This is a really tough problem (I don't trust my team and want to be indispensable).

Lack of delegation is a negative doom loop. Low delegation is seen as low trust, which leads to low motivation, and it also means the team never learns or grows: underperformance is baked in, which then justifies the decision not to delegate.

High delegation is a virtuous circle, signalling high trust, and leads to high motivation and team learning and growth, which enables them to do more and do it better. Hybrid working forces team leaders towards much more delegation than in the past. The three keys to effective delegation are:

The more you delegate, the more you trust your team

- Have the right team.
- Know *what* you can delegate.
- Know *how* you can delegate.

2.1.1 Have the right team

A core task for you as a leader is to pick the right team for the job. If you cannot delegate to your team, then either you have the wrong team or the team has the wrong boss.

Selecting the 'right' team is about values as much as skills. Many bosses find to their cost that they hire for skills and fire for (lack of) values. In practice, you can train skills but you cannot train values. A team member with the right values is someone who:

- You can trust to do the right thing while you are not looking.
- Has the desire to learn and grow, to acquire the skills you need.
- Fits with or complements the values of your team.

Working in the office allows you to compromise on team quality. Because you can see who is struggling (perhaps because they are new in the role), you can shift work to more capable team members and you can provide close support for the struggler. Hybrid working is less forgiving of weak performance. You have to trust that each team member will deliver, without you looking over their shoulder the whole time. Team members understand this intuitively: they know that more autonomy means more accountability. That raises the pressure on them to perform, which is one of the reasons for stress rising during extended periods of WFH.

You can train skills but you cannot train values

2.1.2 Know what you can delegate

Many bosses ask 'what can I delegate?' This is the wrong question. The answer is usually 'very little'. The 'very little' can be a toxic combination of routine rubbish and one or two unpleasant tasks which you want to offload. This sort of delegation is an effective way to demotivate your team.

A better question to ask is 'Is there anything I cannot delegate?' Instead of assuming that you start with all the work yourself, assume that you start with none of the work and then ask 'what do I absolutely have to take away from my team?' Again, the answer will be surprisingly short, if your team is good. You probably have to take performance appraisals away from the team. Beyond that, your list should be short.

The more you delegate, the more you focus your efforts on where you add most value and really make a difference. Delegation makes for more interesting work for yourself, and for your team. The best delegators are often the most effective bosses:

- They show trust in their team, which increases motivation.

- Delegation forces the team to step up and grow their skills and capabilities.
- The team leader has to focus on where he or she can add real value.

If you delegate well you will find that you have to re-invent your role as a leader. Effectively, you have to promote yourself: your title will stay the same, but your role will be different. This is explored later, in Section 2.2.

2.1.3 Know how you can delegate

Many bosses don't delegate for a simple reason: they don't know how to do it. A sure way to demotivate your team is to delegate poorly:

- Delegate only the routine rubbish and one or two nightmare issues.
- Be unclear about what you want and when.
- Change your mind.
- Don't give your team the resources and support they need to succeed.

Turn these problems around and it becomes clear what good delegation looks like. It starts by delegating the right portfolio of work: there will always be dull routine to be delegated, but you should also delegate challenging work which will allow your team to engage and grow.

Be clear about what you want and when. This is exceptionally hard if you have to rely on the written word. You may be able to write down the basics of what is needed by when, but it is nearly impossible to capture all the vital context:

- Who needs it and why do they need it?
- How much detail is required?
- How does this fit with other priorities?
- How does this dovetail with other work?

- Are there any precedents we can use, or no-go areas or must-haves?
- Who else needs to be involved, informed, consulted and who needs to approve what?
- What resources (time, money, budget, political support, access to decision makers and influencers) do you need to set this assignment up for success?

Instead of writing everything down, most bosses correctly discuss the assignment. If it is a significant assignment, it will require much more than one discussion. You will need a series of discussions to discover the whole context. This iterative approach to delegation is messy but effective in the office where it is easy to have a series of short conversations on a topic. WFH makes it much harder to have many small informal discussions.

Delegation is far better suited to the office than to remote working. Working remotely it is easier for misunderstandings to arise, and it takes longer to spot them and fix them. Questions remain unanswered for longer, leading to stress and anxiety. If you have to delegate remotely, do not assume that you can do it via email and do not assume you can do it in one call. Try to replicate the office environment. Instead of having one formal video call to try to cover everything, be ready to call several times during the day for a quick five minute check-up so that any emerging questions and problems can be resolved in near real time.

Be clear about what you want and when

2.2 Recrafting your role as a leader in a world of high autonomy

If you delegate everything, can you delegate yourself out of a job? Is there anything left for you to do? This is the dark fear many managers have, and is one reason they are loth to delegate too much.

In practice, you will find that you have a much more challenging and rewarding role. You create more value by being a good manager than an overpaid supervisor. You have to manage less and lead more. Your team will be grateful that you manage less: that is a sign that you trust them. Leading more forces you to step up. We have already seen that perhaps the most usable definition of leadership is:

Leaders take people where they would not have got by themselves.

Behind this simple definition is a simple agenda which all the best leaders follow: IPM. IPM stands for Idea, People, Money and Machine. Leaders work the agenda in that order: Idea first, then people, then money and machine. Managers work the agenda the other way around: MPI. They are highly fixated on money (managing the budget) and the machine (managing the rhythms and routines of the team). Then they worry about whether they have the right team, and finally they may look at the bigger picture of strategy.

Chapter 3 focuses on people and Chapter 4 focuses on making the machine work when WFH. This section, however, looks at the *Idea* element of IPM.

As a leader, you need to start with your big idea about how you are going to make a difference. If we want to sound sophisticated we can call your idea a strategy, vision or mission. But it all comes down to having an idea about how you will leave your mark. To make it simpler, your idea is nothing more than a story in three parts:

- This is where we are.
- This is where we are going.
- This is how we will get there.

And if you want to make your idea really motivational, you add a fourth element: this is how you can help us get there. This fourth element makes the idea personal and relevant to each member of your team.

'This is where we are' is the problem or opportunity you are going to address. One problem can lead to many different versions of 'This is where we are going'. For instance, if the

Start with your big idea

problem statement is that 'Competition are taking market share from us', you could go in many different directions:

- We will become the lowest cost competitor by restructuring relentlessly.
- We will become the high service firm that everyone wants to deal with.
- We will be the only firm to achieve zero defects to delight and regain customers.
- We will stop worrying about market share: we will ditch unprofitable lines in favour of high profit lines.
- We will innovate our way to success faster than the competition.

The characteristics of a good idea are that it will be:

- Relevant: it addresses a valuable challenge or opportunity.
- Simple: everyone can remember it.
- Stretching: it will not be business as usual. It makes a difference.
- Actionable: everyone will know what they need to do differently.
- Measurable: you will know if and when you have achieved it.

A classic example of a great leader's idea was President Kennedy's promise in 1961 to 'Put a man on the moon by the end of this decade, and bring him back alive again.' It met all the criteria of a strong idea:

- Relevant: the moonshot was to counter the USSR's lead in the space race after they put the first satellite in space (Sputnik) and the first man in space (Yuri Gagarin).
- Simple: going to the moon and back should be easy for most people to remember.
- Stretching: no one had any idea if this was possible or if the technology existed. It was super stretching. As Kennedy added: 'We choose to go to the moon in this decade and do the other things, not because they are easy, but because they are hard; because that goal will serve to organize and measure the best of our energies and skills.'
- Actionable: it was very clear what had to happen. The first thing was to complete the IPM agenda: find the people to do it and find the money and machine to make it happen: NASA was born.
- Measurable: you know if you have been to the moon or not, and it was a time-limited goal: by the end of the 1960s.

You do not need to go to the moon to make a difference. A simple way to find a relevant idea which makes a difference is to listen to what the big boss wants. Conferences where your CEO drones on may be boring, but very useful. They tell you what the CEO is really focused on. For instance, an office manager heard that the Senior Partner of a consulting firm had talked about the need for collaboration and co-operation across all levels of the firm. Because the office manager was not deemed to be important, he had not been allowed to attend the conference. But he heard the message and decided to act on it. He approached the Senior Partner with a plan: rip out all private offices and go to shared working spaces for everyone. The Senior Partner was delighted, especially when she found out how much money this would save. She was less delighted when the office manager suggested that she needed to set an example by moving out of her office into shared space. But she agreed: at that point the office manager had become the leader who was leading everyone, even the Senior Partner. Never underestimate the power of a simple idea.

2.3 Driving change and sustaining the revolution

One big lesson for leaders emerged from the pandemic: people and firms are very agile under the right conditions. In 12 months many firms saw more change than they had seen in as many years and achieved things they would previously have thought impossible. Firms only changed because people moved at warp speed, adapting to WFH and hybrid working often over one weekend. Humans are very agile and resilient when they need to be.

The question is whether this pace of change can be sustained, and how you can sustain it. The pandemic showed how agile we can be. Other times have shown that humans far prefer stability to change. In the last world war, many people went to war and did remarkable things in far off places. They showed huge agility and resilience when necessary. And then they returned

Humans are very agile and resilient when they need to be

to their bungalows in the suburbs and settled down to the quiet life. People prefer stability to change, but can change when they have to.

Leaders have to balance the need for change with the human need for stability, safety and certainty. The first step is to learn why change succeeded so well during the pandemic. You can then apply that learning to sustaining change after the pandemic.

From a firm-wide perspective change succeeds when the following pre-conditions for change exist:

- Need for change is urgent and important (N).
- Vision for the future is articulated (V).
- Capacity and capability exists (C).
- First steps are identified (F).
- Risks of change are mitigated (R).

We can articulate this as a change equation, with all its spurious mathematical accuracy:

$$N + V + C + F > R$$

You can apply this change equation to see if your firm or team is ready to change. The change equation is a reliable predictor of the success or otherwise of change efforts. If the change equation flags problems, it shows you what you need to fix before embarking on change. Here is how the change equation worked at the start of the pandemic:

- *N: Need for change* was acute and important. Working in the office was simply no longer possible because it was outlawed. This is the single most important part of the change equation: pain drives change. If there is no need for change, people will prefer stability and certainty. They will prefer the quiet life in their suburban bungalows to going off to war. You may hear a CEO talk about a 'burning platform': they want to create a sense of crisis in the firm to force the scale and pace of change. Survival is a very strong motivator for change. No one wants to stay on a burning platform. What will be your burning platform after the pandemic is over?

- *V: Vision for change* was largely missing, beyond the most compelling vision of all: we will survive. Normally the vision is aspirational and shows how the world, firm or team will be better after making all the effort of changing things. People want to know that their sacrifice is not in vain and that a better future awaits. Both hope and fear (vision and need) drive change; normally, fear trumps hope.

- *C: Capacity and capability to change.* Change takes effort and skill. You need time, money, political support and staff who can make it happen. One day, none of this existed. Next day, the entire resources of the firm were directed to making change happen, from boardroom to post room. Change is impossible without the capacity and capability to change, but can happen at warp speed when the entire firm is aligned behind it.

- *F: First steps* were immediate and often chaotic: get out of the office and take whatever kit you need with you to set up at home. That was followed by slightly more measured steps such as giving team members allowances to set up home offices, or sending them the kit they needed. First steps matter. They build momentum for change, show that it will work, create a bandwagon effect and encourage the doubters to get on board.

- *R: Risk* is a double-edged sword. There is the risk of doing something, which is why change is resisted. The usual reaction to this is to minimize the perceived risk. There is an alternative: maximize the perceived risk, of doing nothing. Risk is always relative. What is riskier: doing something or doing nothing? If you are on a burning platform, doing nothing is riskier than doing something, like jumping off the platform. With COVID-19, the risk of doing nothing far exceeded the risk of adjusting to a new way of working.

Note how the change equation works at the level of the firm (rational) and at the level of the individual (emotional as well as rational). If the case for change is simply a business case, it does

Pain drives change

not work. Most people really do not wake up excited about going to work in order to increase the firm's stated earnings per share. If you want to make the case for change, you have to make it at both the firm level and at the individual level. These are two entirely different perspectives.

Looking at the change equation for individuals, you have to ask the WIFM question: 'What's In It For Me?' The answer will be different for each person, normally. You have to win hearts and minds one at a time, not with a big PowerPoint presentation to 300 people. Most people will resist change passively rather than overtly. Overt resistance takes effort and is risky. Doing nothing is a simple form of resistance: low effort and low risk. Most people will resist because they will have all sorts of fears about change:

- Will I still have a job? Will I have to move to a new location?
- Will I have to learn new skills?
- Will I have a new boss I may not like?
- Will I have to meet tougher performance standards?

These fears are the real risks of change which sabotage many change efforts. Firms know how to manage rational risks: they appear in risk registers with heat maps and mitigating actions. Rational risks are easy to deal with. The emotional risks of the hopes and fears of each team member are much harder to manage, even when you are in the office. At least in the office you can have frequent, quiet and informal chats with each team member about what change means for them. A video call creates a level of formality and distance which makes it very hard to have a chat in which your team member will disclose their private hopes and fears.

Most people will resist change passively rather than overtly

If you look at the change equation from the perspective of one of your team members, it becomes clear why change happened fast. The change equation itself changes and adapts to reflect the perspective of the individual.

- *N: Need to change.* 'The office is being closed down: help! What do I need to do to survive, to keep my job?'
- *V: Vision for change.* 'Keeping my job would be a great vision for my future. And WFH sounds like a nice idea: no more commuting.' (Or for some: 'WFH sounds like hell given I am in a noisy flat share with nowhere to work, but at least I keep my job').
- *C: Capacity and capability to change* for the individual is about another C: control. If people have control or influence over their destiny, they will experience less anxiety and they will be more likely to embrace change. If change is being done to them and they have no control over their future, then fear, perceived risk and resistance to change rises fast. This change was empowering because firms had no time to tell people what to do or how to do it. Everyone had to figure out how to make it work for themselves.
- *F: First steps:* 'I need to grab my office laptop and everything else I need to set up at home.' It was very clear what needed to happen.

- *R: Risks of change.* 'WFH may be a crazy concept, but the risk of doing nothing is far greater with both the office and public transport being shut down.'

The change equation shows why so much change happened so fast at the start of the pandemic. The challenge is whether you can sustain that change. If you run the change equation for your firm, and then for your team members, you will come up with a very different answer: the appetite for sustained change probably does not exist.

The challenge of change is greater with hybrid working. The change equation implies, correctly, that making change happen means that you have to build a coalition in support of change. At the best of times, it is hard to build the coalition because the firm is full of conflicting interests. Your vision of change may carry great benefits to your team, but be a huge risk or diversion of resources for another team. During the pandemic everyone saw the change equation the same way and made the same calculation. During normal times, different teams, functions, geographies and business units will have different interests and different calculations.

In practice, all firms are set up for conflict. This is a surprise to many business gurus who see firms as islands of co-operation which minimize transaction costs. In practice, healthy competition between competing groups and ideas in the firm help decide the priorities of the firm and where resources will be allocated. Your biggest competition may be sitting at a hot desk near you, competing for the same limited pot of budget, resources, support, bonuses and promotions.

Your biggest competition may be sitting at a hot desk near you

The office is the perfect battleground for ideas and groups to compete. There are endless opportunities for informal discussions with influencers and decision makers. This lets you build your coalition, identify and deal with obstacles and objections and discover who represents the real threat to your agenda. If this sounds political, it is: firms are deeply political organizations. The more senior you become, the more political your job becomes. Politics in this sense is not a dirty word. Politics is about how you make the organization you work for, work for you. You have to find ways of promoting your agenda, securing resources and support for your priorities.

Coalition building in a political world means that decisions are taken in the corridor, not in the boardroom. By the time a decision goes to the board, you should know what the answer will be. The Japanese have a word for this: *nemawashi*. This is the art of building consensus before the decision-making meeting: agreements are reached in private and the formal meeting serves only to make public the private agreements. *Nemawashi* works very well when you have frequent and informal encounters with colleagues in corridors. It becomes very hard when you have to set up a formal Zoom meeting: an informal and flexible chat quickly becomes a formal negotiation in which positions are taken. Once a colleague takes a position, they tend to stick with it and confirmation bias creeps in: they interpret every new piece of information as confirmation that their original position was correct.

Decisions are taken in the corridor, not in the boardroom

How can you go about coalition building, influencing decisions and starting change in a hybrid world?

The simple answer is to get into the office more often, especially when key stakeholders are there. That is where you can engineer chance encounters with the people you need to speak with. You can have informal discussions which help you navigate the political waters of your firm, build your informal coalition and set up the decision you want made. Corridor talk is also an excellent way of gathering intelligence about what the CEO is really thinking, who is planning what, where the opportunities and death traps lie. You can get some of this from instant messaging and video calls, but disclosure tends to be richer and more honest when it is in person.

If WFH is essential, you have to find other ways of gathering intelligence and building support. You have three lines of defence for this:

1. *Stick closely to the CEO's agenda.* What the CEO wants, the CEO gets. The weak form of alignment is to ensure that what you are proposing aligns with the CEO's agenda. The strong form is to make sure that the CEO knows you are aligned with her agenda, and to get her endorsement for what you are doing. Suddenly, all the opposition to your idea will melt away: opponents may want to take you on, but taking on the CEO is normally a CLM: Career Limiting Move. The implication is that hybrid working makes command and control easier in strategic terms and in deciding the direction and priorities of the firm. Day to day command and control remains harder for managers who cannot see or hear their teams all day.

2. *Work your network of trust.* In Chapter 1 we saw how you can build your network of trust. You need a few trusted people who you can rely on to tell you what is happening, what is being planned and who is thinking what. Call them and call in some favours from them. Then be sure to reciprocate: trust is a two-way street based on mutual interests which you have to sustain.

3. *Engineer informal discussions with key stakeholders.* Every formal meeting is the chance for an informal discussion. In the office, the most important part of many meetings often happens just before and just after the formal meeting, where you have private discussions with the person you need to help you.

Online, it is nearly impossible to have a private chat before or after a meeting if there are several people at the meeting. Before the meeting, everyone else is there and can hear your 'private' discussion. At the end there is no time for informal chat because everyone logs off and rushes to the next call.

You have to engineer a one-to-one call, which might ostensibly be on another topic. You can then informally raise your real issue in the informal chat at the start of the call. When meeting in person, it is often best to raise the real issue at the end of the meeting when your colleague is relaxing after finishing the formal business. Online, he will be rushing to the next meeting at the end of your call, so you have to raise your issue at the start. This is necessary, not ideal.

The nature of change shows the power of the office. The office enables more and better communication, informal communication, intelligence gathering, access to key influencers and decision makers, trust building and coalition building in a way which WFH does not. Difficult conversations are even more difficult when you are remote.

There is one other area where intelligence gathering, access to key influencers and decision makers and having difficult conversations is vital: managing your career. This is why:

- *Intelligence gathering*: the office rumour mill is vital in telling you what opportunities are emerging, which are the death star assignments to avoid and which boss is worth working for.
- *Access to key influencers and decision makers*. Having HR onside helps when it comes to assignment time, and being able to talk to a potential future boss always helps

you: you can decide whether you want to be available and make a good impression on the new boss by helping out, or whether you mysteriously want to become completely unavailable for that boss's assignments.

- *Difficult conversations* about careers, expectations and performance are best done early and informally when you can take action and correct course if necessary.

Sustaining the status quo and sustaining your job is very doable WFH. But if you want to make real change and build your career, the office is where you need to be. Hybrid working may allow you to make the best of both worlds if you manage the balance between WFH and office work properly.

Difficult conversations are even more difficult when you are remote

2.4 Key points

1. WFH increases autonomy, which walks hand in hand with increased accountability.
2. Professionals and remote working do not go well with micromanagement: manage better by managing less.
3. Don't ask 'What can I delegate?' Ask 'what can I not delegate?' The answer to both questions is 'very little'.
4. Refocus your role on leadership: 'Leaders take people where they would not have got by themselves'.
5. WFH showed that firms, teams and people are capable of far more change than we previously thought. Be bolder in taking on change.
6. Two main barriers to change are:
   - People prefer stability to change, normally.
   - WFH is well suited to stable situations, not to rapid change.

7. Set up the pre-conditions for change in your team:
   - Need: show that there is a need for change.
   - Vision: show how the change will lead to a better place for your team.
   - Capacity and Capability has to be in place to succeed.
   - First steps to build momentum, gain some wins, get the bandwagon moving.
   - Risk, especially emotional and political risk, derails change: manage it by reducing the perceived risk of action or increasing the perceived risk of inaction.

3

Motivation, mental health and mastery to sustain peak performance

WFH has led to a quiet pandemic of mental health challenges. Team leaders cannot be counsellors to their team, nor can they order their team to be motivated. But you can create the conditions in which your team will discover their intrinsic motivation, and in which they will acquire the resilience to help themselves thrive and sustain high performance.

This chapter explores how you can:

- *Create the conditions in which you and your team will thrive.*
- *Manage your inner world to sustain your health and performance.*
- *Motivate yourself and your team.*

3.0 Motivation and the mental health challenge of WFH

If you feel that you have suffered WFH, you are not alone. There has been a quiet epidemic of mental ill health as a result of WFH. Nuffield Health has stated that over 80 per cent of people report that their mental health has suffered when working from home. This is not surprising:

- We are social animals, and we are not at our best when cut off from our social and professional networks.
- Loss of boundaries between home and work life means that we never switch off properly and never recharge our batteries.

You cannot perform at your best if you do not feel at your best. You need to manage both your outer world (the conditions you work in) and your inner world (how you react to your conditions).

WFH has led to a quiet pandemic of mental health challenges

In the past, many firms ignored mental health issues. Staff learned to keep their mental health issues to themselves, because it was regarded as a sign of weakness. WFH forced firms to start taking mental health seriously, because so many high performers struggled when cut off from the social structure and rhythms and routines of the office.

As ever, prevention is far better than cure. Effective prevention is about creating the conditions where staff thrive and:

- Re-discover their intrinsic motivation for their job.
- Build resilience in the good times to help them through the hard times.
- Sustain high performance not for a few weeks but for decades.

Counselling services and professional help are a necessary last line of defence in dealing with mental health issues. Using the last line of defence implies that the first lines of defence have failed. It is better to have a first line of defence that works: if you are a leader, you are the first line of defence.

This chapter is about how you can be an effective first line of defence in promoting motivation and sustaining high performance: you can help prevent, but you cannot cure, mental health challenges. A team member who is motivated and enjoying work is less likely to suffer than someone who is disengaged. Your focus is on the positive agenda of helping your team discover their intrinsic motivation for what they do.

3.1 Create the conditions in which you and your team will thrive

There are two things you can do as the first line of defence in promoting motivation, performance and wellbeing:

- Be a role model.
- Fix the plumbing: put in place the right infrastructure rhythms and routines.

3.1.1 Be a role model

As the team leader you set the values for your team by how you act. If you are attempting to work 24/7 that is not good for you, and it is not good for the team: they will think that they have to keep up with you. Set clear time boundaries and show that you adhere to them. If that means you take time off to do the school run or take exercise

We remember what people are like more than what they do

at lunchtime, do not hide the fact. Be clear and let everyone know that is your routine. The chances are that you make up for the lost time by working a few hours very early or late: make it clear that is personal work time, not collaboration time.

As an exercise, try to recall how well your first boss met her objectives. Now try recalling what she was like. We remember what people are like more than what they do. And that applies to you: colleagues will remember how you are, not what you did. You are a role model for your team, for better or for worse.

If you want your team to feel good and do well, you cannot tell them to be positive, or happy. But you can be a positive role model. Being positive does not mean chanting 'Have a nice day' to everyone you meet, although that may help. It is about showing positive behaviours, especially at difficult moments.

The table below frames the choices for you: what sort of boss do you want to work for, and what sort of boss do you want to be?

Negative behaviour	Positive behaviour
Focus on problems	Focus on solutions
Analyse what happened	Drive to action
Look back	Look to the future
Seek to criticize	Seek to praise
New ideas are risky	New ideas are opportunities

Normally, behaviours are a symptom of how you think. But causality can also run the other way. By forcing yourself to adopt positive behaviours, you force yourself to think positively as well. This is less intimidating for your team members:

Positive behaviour leads to positive thinking

changing behaviours is about good teamwork, changing the way they think is messing with their heads and they will resist it. But positive behaviour leads to positive thinking.

The key is to be relentless and consistent in your behaviour pattern. If you praise 95 per cent of the time but then criticize when things go awry for 5 per cent of the time, you will be seen as a critical boss, not a supportive boss. Only when you are 100 per cent consistent will your team realize that they need to adjust their behaviour.

By role modelling the behaviour you want, you get the behaviour you want. This is clearly an advantage of the office where you live life like a goldfish in a bowl: everyone can observe everything you do and can learn from it. WFH makes it much harder to be a role model, positive or otherwise, for your team.

WFH you have to create the framework in which you and your team can sustain their motivation to feel good and function well. You can create these conditions for your team whether they are remote, hybrid or office based.

3.1.2 Fix the plumbing: get the right infrastructure rhythms and routines

Fixing the plumbing is about creating the right rhythms, routines and infrastructure to enable yourself and your team to flourish. These are covered in full in Chapter 4.

You have to look after yourself if you are to look after your team or colleagues. If you are struggling personally, you will have limited capacity to help anyone else. Here are the essential lessons about how you can create the right conditions for yourself:

- *Create time boundaries* between home and work.
- *Create physical boundaries* between home and work.
- *Have clear goals* to be productive and to have a clear finish to the day.
- *Reach out*. Gossip is good: social bonds help build teams.

- *Take exercise.* A walking phone call can be better than a video call from a desk.

Exactly the same messages apply to you in your role as a team leader. You have to role model that you are doing what you expect your team to do:

- *Create time boundaries,* and honour them yourself. Don't communicate 24/7.
- *Create physical boundaries.* Make sure your team have the technical set up for WFH.
- *Have clear goals.* Avoid ambiguity which causes stress, and easily arises from WFH.
- *Reach out.* Take time to check-in with each team member. Working remotely, you can't see if they are struggling and they may not want to complain: ask them.
- *Take exercise.* Even a standing meeting (all stand up) is better than everyone sitting down all day.

As a boss, you need a team which has commitment, not just compliance. That means you need to be the boss your team wants to work for, not has to work for. WFH makes the challenge even harder, because it is hard to build trust and relationships remotely.

Be the boss your team wants to work for, not has to work for

But there is one thing you can do, which I discovered from extensive research to find out what made a good manager from the point of view of the team. Out of more than 100 questions, one stood out as the golden question which predicted accurately whether the boss would be seen to have all the good qualities of a manager: insight, competence, motivation skills and even sense of humour. Here is the golden question you have to answer if you want to be seen as a great boss by your team:

'My manager cares for me and my career' (agree/disagree on a 5-point scale)

If you can show you care for a team member, he will believe that you are a great manager. Reaching out and showing you care is not about being nice: caring can involve difficult but constructive conversations about performance and career development.

3.2 Manage your inner world to sustain your health and performance

An old adage claims that leadership is lonely. At first sight, the adage is nonsense: leaders are always surrounded by people and are in constant meetings. How can they be lonely? In truth, you can be lonely in a crowd. As a leader, everyone wants a piece of your time; everyone comes to you with their agenda and they want more support, more resources, more of your time. There is no such thing as an open discussion and it is hard to relax. There is no one you can turn to when you want to vent your feelings or even just gossip. Leaders do not have a shoulder to cry on.

WFH makes the challenge worse: not only does the leader have no one to lean on, everyone else wants to lean on the leader. Informal chats with your senior colleagues become hard when you are remote from them. As a leader, your first task is to look after yourself. If you cannot look after yourself, you cannot look after your team. You need a good inner game to sustain your resilience, motivation and performance.

If you cannot look after yourself, you cannot look after your team

Your inner game is about how you react to the world around you. The first and most important insight is that you can choose how you react to your world. Optimists and pessimists live in the same world, but react to it in fundamentally different ways. Our reactions are deeply ingrained habits which we learn over a lifetime. As with all habits, they can be helpful or unhelpful. We can keep our helpful habits and adjust unhelpful habits if we have enough determination.

The habits which matter are the way we manage our internal chatter. We can be cruel to ourselves, saying things we would never say to colleagues. The goal is to make sure you are your own best friend, not your own worst critic, in your internal chatter. WFH there are some clear dos and don'ts.

Don't	Do
Ruminate	Reach out
Catastrophize	Stay positive
Mind read	Enquire

3.2.1 Don't ruminate, do reach out

Imagine that you are in a team meeting and your boss says something which could be seen as critical of your work. In the office, you can deal with this fairly quickly. You may be able to have a quiet word with your boss after the meeting to find out what was really intended. If that is not possible, you will have colleagues who will happily fill in the blanks for you. The office gossip machine will give you a range of views: one person might take delight in catastrophizing for you; another might dismiss it all as a non-event and a third colleague might actually shed some constructive light on the comment for you. Crucially, you will not be alone. You will be able to hear a range of opinions which help you form a fairly balanced view of where you stand.

Imagine the same thing happens, except that you are WFH and on a video call. You cannot corner your boss after the meeting. You will not hear what anyone else thinks. You will be left to work it out for yourself. From there, it is easy to start ruminating on what was said. You start to imagine all the different scenarios which might play out. As humans are risk averse, a natural survival instinct is to work out all the negative scenarios and how you might deal with them. After a day and a long night ruminating about it, you may start to see the really dark side. You start catastrophizing: the project is doomed, you will be fired, in hard times you can't get another job, you cannot afford the mortgage and you will be begging on the streets. All because your boss used loose language to describe your project.

It is all too easy to ruminate at home, and rumination is rarely positive. The antidote is to reach out. Reaching out deals not just with the problem of rumination: it also helps sustain your mental health more broadly. You have three resources for reaching out:

- Friends and family. A problem shared is a problem halved, and a joy shared is a joy doubled. Just talking things through with friends and family provides balance and perspective. The sharing is two way: you help them as much as they help you if you reach out to them. At times when people are isolated, make the extra effort to connect with them.
- Colleagues and bosses. Colleagues provide the antidote to your rumination. They know the context and the players, unlike friends and family. They give you an alternative perspective on how things are. Colleagues comfort each other in the face of the enemy, which is usually the boss, not the competition.

- Professional help. The good news is that the stigma attached to mental health issues is vanishing. Because everyone suffered somewhat during the pandemic, bosses and firms realize that they have to take mental health seriously. Most firms now offer help lines and access to professional help. Like seeing your doctor, the earlier you go the better. Prevent the problem if you can, fix it fast if you can. Don't let it fester; don't let a small problem become a big crisis.

3.2.2 Don't catastrophize, do stay positive

From rumination to catastrophizing is a small step. You know you are catastrophizing when you use absolute words such as 'Never, no one, always, everyone, nothing.' If you start telling yourself 'My boss always undermines me, nothing works with him and no one supports me....' you are in a bad place, which is hard to escape. If you catastrophize, you will find plenty of evidence to support your contention that your boss undermines you, nothing works and no one supports you. This is confirmation bias: we look for evidence which supports our view, and disregard evidence which contradicts it.

A problem shared is a problem halved, and a joy shared is a joy doubled

The best way to deal with catastrophizing is to prevent it. Fortunately, it is very easy to spot if you stay alert. As soon as you start using absolute words (no one, never, nothing), that should raise a red flag in your mind: you are starting to catastrophize. Tell yourself that you are catastrophizing and that you are about to fall into the confirmation bias trap: you are in danger of looking for all the evidence which supports your view of catastrophe. Already, you are halfway to success. Now force yourself to look for evidence that 'No one, never, nothing' is not entirely true. As contradictory evidence builds, you can start to take a more balanced view of your situation.

An even better way of avoiding catastrophizing is to stay positive. I was brought up to believe that the only reason it is not raining is because it is about to rain: I was a fully trained pessimist. I was shocked to discover that you can choose to be pessimistic or optimistic. I was even more shocked to find that optimists live longer and do better than pessimists. So I decided I had to figure out this optimism gig. Here is the recovering pessimist's guide to optimism and positive thinking:

- Recognize that optimism and pessimism, being positive and negative, is a choice. Optimists live longer and do better, so choose well.
- Optimism is not about hoping to get lucky, because hope is not a method and luck is not a strategy. Positive thinking embraces the brutal facts, however unpleasant they may be, and finds ways to overcome or mitigate the brutal facts. Drive to action and focus on the future: don't look back, don't ruminate and don't start the blame game. This is a version of optimism which is highly effective in the workplace, especially when times are hard.
- Count your blessings. The following exercise has repeatedly been proven to work. At the end of each day, write down three good things about the day. Repeat for 30 days. Soon you start noticing all the good things in life and it becomes a habit. The pessimist's version of writing down all the rubbish things that happened in the day is a shortcut to misery. Alternative versions of this exercise include writing down three ways you helped other people or were helped; or writing down

three things you learned in the day. The act of writing matters: it makes it a conscious and deliberate process. You train your brain to look at the world differently.

- See your world differently. This is an instant version of count your blessings. Answer one question: would you rather be a prince or princess 300 years ago, or live life today with all its challenges? When groups answer this, 95 per cent elect to stay with today – 300 years ago meant no indoor sanitation, no running water, no central heating, no electricity or internet, no painkillers, no dental care, no antibiotics and you might bath once a year. Royalty looked heavenly and smelled to high heaven. If we are better off than royalty used to be, life cannot be all bad.

3.2.3 Don't mind read, do enquire

A sure way to have a bad conversation is to try mind reading:

- 'You don't really mean that…'
- 'You're not really sorry…'
- 'What you really mean is…'
- 'You don't really care…'

There is no positive end to such a start. If you disagree with the mind reader, the mind reader takes that as evidence that they are right. If you agree with them, you are in the bad place they want to put you in.

The message about mind reading is simple: don't do it, unless you want to spoil a relationship.

Unfortunately, remote working encourages mind reading.

Hope is not a method and luck is not a strategy

Because you are not in constant, close contact with your colleagues you have plenty of time to ruminate over what colleagues did or didn't say or do. Mind reading is a natural by-product of ruminating. As you ruminate, it is easy to start assigning meanings to what was said and feelings and intentions to people you work with. If your analysis is accurate, that can help you find a solution. If it is inaccurate, it makes the problem worse.

The solution to mind reading is the same as the solution to rumination: reach out and enquire. Do not rely only on your own judgement, which is limited by the information you have. Other colleagues will have more information and alternative perspectives.

If you think that a colleague is saying things which are different from what they really think or intend to do, don't leap to assumptions. Confirm and clarify with them what they mean.

- Confirm: the simplest way to confirm what they mean is to paraphrase back to them what they said. 'So what you are saying is....' If you are correct, you are both happy. If you are incorrect, you will both see the problem and rectify it. Paraphrasing is a useful art: it forces you to listen accurately; it confirms mutual understanding and gives your colleague confidence that you have understood their meaning. It is also neutral and non-judgemental. It sets up a more constructive conversation than mind reading.
- Clarify: this goes one step further than confirming. You clarify by exploring the consequences of what has been proposed. If your boss changes a deadline on you, explore why there is a change and what consequences the new deadline will have, for instance in changing other priorities and deadlines. By stress testing a colleague's statement you discover what was really intended without resorting to the paranormal magic of mind reading.

Most office feuds are the result of misunderstandings or the clash of personal styles. Remote working reduces the impact of differing styles, but increases the chances of misunderstanding. Be more purposeful and more deliberate in how you communicate and listen. Preventing misunderstanding is always better than trying to cure it after the event.

3.3 Motivate yourself and your team

You only excel at what you enjoy because success requires sustained effort and extra effort. You have to step up for the special project where you learn new skills, you have to put in extra hours to help out in a crisis, you have to go the extra yard to turn a good presentation into a great presentation. Simply doing your job is not enough to progress. Success is built on endless discretionary effort. Your career is a marathon, not a sprint. To succeed, you need the will to put in extra hours not just for a few weeks, but for a few decades. You can only do that if you enjoy what you do.

In the short term, professionals can sustain extra effort to deal with a crisis. That is what has happened in the early stages of the pandemic. The response was a tribute to the commitment and motivation of all professionals. But when the second lockdown came, the motivation was no longer there. The excitement and novelty of dealing with the crisis had gone, and all that was left was the long grind of working in isolation and morale plummeted in many firms. Once the crisis is over, you need to find another way of sustaining the motivation of your team.

While many people enjoyed WFH, many others suffered, especially if they were isolated, or had poor conditions for WFH. WFH and hybrid working forces managers to be more conscious and deliberate in how they motivate their team.

There are, broadly, two ways to motivate yourself and your team: extrinsic or intrinsic.

- *Extrinsic motivation* involves things like money and working conditions. They were the staple of trade union negotiations for decades. The negotiations normally led to unhappy workers, not happy workers. At the other extreme, money is clearly a motivator in some industries such as investment banking. The problem with the money motivator is the hedonic treadmill: the more you have, the more you want. You find that you have to run faster and faster just to keep up. There is always something more you want, especially as you will be surrounded by peers and bosses who already have something more than you. Stepping off the treadmill is hard: once you are used to the champagne and caviar lifestyle it is hard to go back to living on pies and pints of beer. And as for the horror of having to turn right at the aircraft door....
- *Intrinsic motivation* lasts longer but is harder to build. Intrinsic motivation is about having a strong inner drive to do your job, regardless of extrinsic drivers such as pay and conditions. Organizations with some of the most committed staff have some of the poorest extrinsic motivators. The army, church and voluntary organizations are full of very committed people working on low pay and often in poor conditions.

This section is about how you can find intrinsic motivation for yourself. The goal is to wake up in the morning wanting to work, not having to work. The essence of intrinsic motivation comes down to another version of RAMP, which we can call mini-RAMP or motivation-RAMP.

- Relationships, which are supportive.
- Autonomy.
- Mastery.
- Purpose.

Think about the times you have felt most motivated and the chances are that they follow the RAMP principle. You will have had good relationships with your colleagues; you will have been trusted by your boss who gave you autonomy and freedom to get on with the job; you would have had the skills to perform the job and may have learned new skills as well; your work will have had meaning and purpose.

Motivation matters for your performance, and for the performance of those you lead. I asked a school class if they had ever been taught by an unhappy teacher. A forest of small arms shot up in the air. I asked them to describe what it was like. The broad summary: it was miserable. Everyone knows when the boss is unhappy and it is good for no one. You can only motivate your team if you are motivated yourself. As a motivated team leader, your task is to help your team discover their intrinsic motivation. You cannot tell them to be happy or motivated, but you can create the conditions in which they will flourish.

You can only motivate your team if you are motivated yourself

The RAMP model implies that we should start our journey with supportive relationships. However, this journey starts with Purpose. Motivation without purpose is very hard to achieve. Although we start with purpose, the model remains RAMP. Calling it the PRAM model really does not work at all.

3.3.1 Find your purpose: the art of job crafting

It is easy to feel motivated when we strive for a meaningful personal goal or when we feel that we are part of something bigger and worthwhile. Ideally, we have both a meaningful personal goal and we feel we are part of something bigger.

People who have a strong personal goal often have strong intrinsic motivation. Airport bookshelves heave with inspirational books by mountaineers, athletes and entrepreneurs who all tell their stories of how they overcame overwhelming odds and extreme adversity to achieve their personal goal. While these books are entertaining, they are not always helpful. Ultimately, these are selfish stories of people going to great lengths to achieve their personal goals. A team that is full of people going to great lengths to achieve their personal goals is likely to be highly dysfunctional, unless the team is all trying to achieve the same goal, such as win a sports tournament.

Within a team, you have to find a goal that is meaningful to you and that helps the team. This is called job crafting: see your job in a different way from the bland job description you have, to make it meaningful. Three examples will make the point.

Example 1: finding meaning as a hospital cleaner

Hospital cleaners are at the bottom of the pyramid. In hospitals doctors are gods, nurses are angels, cleaners are invisible. They are only noticed when there is a problem. Their pay is as poor as their status, and they often work long hours to make ends meet. So how can you find meaning in a demeaning job?

Sonia made use of the fact that she was ignored by the doctors and nurses. As she did her cleaning round she would pass all the patients. Some would want to be left to themselves, but many wanted a chat, that was not just a medical conversation. As she talked, she saw that lonely and isolated patients would cheer up. And then COVID-19 hit. Suddenly, patients were more isolated, lonely and frightened than ever. And cleaning was more important than ever.

Sonia no longer sees her job as cleaning. She is saving lives by cleaning and boosting morale by talking. She is in the job of changing lives and loves it.

Example 2: find meaning as a hate figure

Since the GFC (Great Financial Crisis) of 2007–08 bankers have been widely loathed for their perceived greed in creating the crisis. So who do the bankers hate? They hate their risk officers. Risk officers spoil the bankers' party by stopping them taking insane risks which might earn a bonus this year but cost the bank a fortune next year. So why would you want to get up every morning when you are hated by the people that everyone else hates?

David was CRO (Chief Risk Officer) of a large bank. He saw his job positively: 'The GFC was a disaster. It led to 10 years of austerity and suffering, it encouraged extremists and populists, it nearly destroyed capitalism and society as we know it. My job is to stop this ever happening again. My job is to save the bank and save the nation from disaster. Who wouldn't want to go to work in the morning when their job is to save the country?'

One of these examples comes from the bottom of the job pyramid, the other from the top of the pyramid. They both used the same technique to craft their jobs positively. They asked themselves: 'who am I helping and where am I making a difference?' In both cases, they found meaning which did not exist in the job description.

To craft your job ask 'who am I helping and where am I making a difference?' The immediate answer may be that you are helping your boss and you are making a difference by meeting budget goals, but that is not inspiring. You have to look further to your end customers. For instance, for many years Federal Express ran a campaign with staff based on the 'golden package'.

As staff sorted parcels or did their rounds, they never knew what was in each package, but one package might be the package that changes someone's life forever. That meant staff had to treat every package like it might be the life-changing package. Consequently, drivers often went to great lengths to ensure that every package would be delivered on time. Delivering parcels is a job, changing lives is a calling.

Example 3: the stone masons

The final example is the age-old fable of the three medieval construction workers, building a cathedral that they would never live to see completed. A visitor asked them what they were doing.

- The first, miserable, worker replied: 'I hack at stones all day.'
- The second worker looked more engaged and replied: 'I am a master mason, carving with all the skill I have learned over the years.'
- The third worker was positively enthusiastic about what he did and replied: 'I am also a master mason and I am building a monument to God. It is a legacy which will inspire countless generations that come after me.'

All three apocryphal masons had the same job of hacking at stones all day, but they saw it in completely different ways. Are you hacking at stones or leaving a legacy for the future?

Are you hacking at stones or leaving a legacy for the future?

3.3.2 Build supportive relationships

Leadership today is a team sport. You cannot do it all yourself, which is great news. You don't need to be good at everything and you do not need to get ticks in all the boxes. Focus on your strengths and let others focus on their strengths. If you hate accounting, learn to love accountants: they will do what you prefer not to do.

The importance of supportive relationships only increases with remote and hybrid working. Isolation leads to low morale, especially for anyone who is an extrovert. But even if you can sustain your morale when working remotely, supportive relationships are still vital for teamwork. A supportive relationship is always based on trust, and no team can function well unless team members trust each other. Building trust was the focus of Chapter 1. Here, we will focus on how you can support colleagues, and how you can encourage them to support you.

Leadership today is a team sport

Supportive relationships are both emotional and practical. Emotionally, we occasionally need someone to lean on. Office life is full of minor injustices inflicted on us by bosses and colleagues. It is good to be able to vent frustration to someone who understands and empathizes. But you also need practical support: you need colleagues who will help you out when you are in a corner, you need a boss who will mind your back and give you political cover when you need it.

You have to build supportive relationships in the good times so that they can carry you through the tough times. Fix the roof while the sun shines. In a crisis, you need to know who you can turn to. As a colleague, there are three things you can do to build supportive relationships:

1. Reach out and listen.
2. Respond appreciatively.
3. Help out.

1. Reach out and listen

In the office, this is easy. Stand by the water cooler long enough and you will meet everyone in that part of the office. You may not get any work done, but at least you will have talked to everyone. Water cooler chat is informal: it may be about work or life, but it is a good way to get to know people. All you have to do is listen. Look at how two people gossip in a coffee shop: all it takes to keep one person talking is for the other person to look interested and occasionally say things like: 'really!?…what??…no!?…he didn't, did he?' By listening you learn what makes the other person tick. You also delight the speaker, because people like speaking about their favourite subject: themselves.

Reaching out informally is much harder remotely. This is one of the reasons why hybrid working will prevail over pure remote working. At some point, people need to be together to interact informally and socially and to build the bonds of trust which will help them in tough times. Many teams attempt to recreate the banter with Slack groups or with online team events which are social in purpose. These can help sustain existing relationships, but do little to help new team members create the relationships they need to become fully effective.

2. Respond appreciatively

Research shows that there is no point at which flattery becomes counterproductive. This sits alongside research showing that the vast majority of the population think that they are above average. I occasionally ask groups how many people think that they are below average in terms of:

- Honesty.
- Effort.
- Competence.
- Teamwork.

Virtually no one is brave enough to say that they are below average. Everyone thinks that they are above average: this is statistically impossible but emotionally inevitable. We are all heroes of our own life journey, although few people truly recognize our worth. This means that it is wonderful when someone appears to recognize our contribution and abilities as much as we do. Naturally, we are inclined to respect and admire someone with such fine judgement: we have just let ourselves fall for the charms of flattery.

Colleagues crave praise. But you have to do it the right way. Being condescending is a disaster: 'well done, you came in with polished shoes today' will not go down well. Here are two situations where you can respond positively in a way that builds a good relationship:

We are all heroes of our own life journey

Situation 1: a colleague has been helpful

'Thank you' is simple to say and much underused, so use it more. The best way to say thank you is to make it a rich thank you. Show how your colleague has made a difference to you personally: perhaps she saved you time, or her work helped you impress a client, or she provided an insight you did not expect. The more your gratitude is personal and specific, the better it is.

Expressing thanks is an easy way to store up goodwill for the days when you may need it.

Situation 2: a colleague has done great work

Imagine a team member comes to you with news that he has just closed a big sale. There are four ways you could respond:

- Active negative: 'You did what? Don't you realize we are fully booked as it is? Where is your risk assessment? Have you got all the approvals? Are you insane?'

- Passive negative: 'Oh? Everyone is getting big sales at the moment. Sandra has just reported a huge sale, much bigger than yours.'
- Passive positive (without looking up from your work): 'Oh well done. Let sales operations know, please. They need the paperwork.'
- Active positive: Stop what you are doing, focus all your attention on your colleague, praise constructively and then let your colleague relish his success. Ask him what happened and how he did it. By doing this, you are both learning about what works, but you are also letting him enjoy his success to the full. All you have to do is to ask constructive questions and listen.

Active positive responding is your chance to build a positive relationship in the sunny days, which will help you on the rainy days to come.

3. Help out

Supportive relationships are a two-way street. If you want support, you have to give support. This does not mean you have to work all night and all day. Support can be quick, focused and decisive.

Helping out is about being a good colleague and team member. You can help out by:

- Being reliable: doing as you say.
- Answering emails promptly.
- Being available for advice and support.
- Supporting your colleague in a crisis.
- Praising her contribution in public.
- Volunteering for a project for your boss.

You do not need to be altruistic to offer help. Helping out is a good way of furthering your own self-interest. Human nature is to want to reciprocate favours; as social animals we want to build bonds in the good times that will help us in the hard times. Throughout history, much gift giving has been highly ritualized. Henry VIII of England had it down to a fine art. At Christmas he gave out lavish gifts to all the bishops and peers and the value of each gift reflected the value of each recipient. A few days later, all the bishops and peers would assemble to offer their gifts in return and in public. Henry VIII usually made a profit on the gift-giving season: no courtier would risk the displeasure of the king by being mean. Reciprocity is normally more informal and natural because no one wants to be the office Scrooge.

This tit for tat principle matters. If you keep on giving and you get nothing in return, you are being exploited. Worse, you set the expectation that you will work extra hours for free: effectively you announce to the world that your time is worthless. If you find that there is a colleague who is unreliable and does not return favours, quietly direct your favour and your efforts in another direction.

Working remotely makes it easy to hide, and hard to shine. There are fewer spontaneous interactions than there are in the office, that means that there are fewer opportunities to see where you can help out. You cannot see when your colleague needs help, so you can hide and focus on your own needs. This reduced visibility is also your opportunity. If you call colleagues unprompted for a chat, most will be delighted and surprised. As you talk, there will normally be some small favour you realize that you

Working remotely makes it easy to hide, and hard to shine

could do for them: do that and you will stand out as one of the few people who are going the extra distance to be helpful. Turn the challenge of WFH to your advantage.

3.3.3 Autonomy and accountability

The psychological contract between employer and employee has been slowly shifting for decades. In the days of Scientific Management, 100 years ago, the bosses had the brains and the workers had the hands. The job of the boss was to get their ideas into the hands of the workers and tell them precisely what to do. Workers were not meant to think for themselves; thinking and doing were different jobs, but education changed all that. Professionals do not need to be told exactly how to do their job. Although many bosses still enjoy a command and control way of working, it is becoming ever harder to sustain in the face of a professional workforce who often know better than the boss how things should be done.

The move to hybrid working dramatically accelerated the shift from command and control. The result is that professionals have more autonomy than ever before, but they also have more accountability than ever before. Professionals enjoy the autonomy but are less certain about enjoying the accountability. The challenge is to make sure you can enjoy the increase in both autonomy and accountability.

In the old world of low autonomy, you had to follow the process and do as you were told even if it did not make much sense. In the new world of high accountability and high autonomy you have to focus on results. It is not enough to turn up and follow the process: you have to show results.

Results focus is the dark side of autonomy. Remote working made results focus particularly difficult for many professionals. In the office, you have a constant informal dialogue with your boss and your colleagues. They can see you are working, and you can constantly shape their expectations about what you are doing and what they should expect from you. Working from home changed all this:

- Your boss cannot see how hard or how long you work.

- You cannot informally adjust and shape your boss's expectations about what you should achieve and by when.

WFH means you cannot prove you are working and you are uncertain what good looks like. If you are a dedicated professional who likes to overachieve, that is a recipe for paranoia, stress and overwork. That is exactly what many professionals experienced WFH. Far from autonomy being liberating and motivating, they found that it was a stressful burden.

The key to unlocking this problem is to lean into the challenge of being results focused. That means you have to do two things:

1. Be crystal clear about what success looks like: define the end goal.
2. Set yourself up for success before you start.

If you do those two things you double down on accountability, which will please the boss. But you also remove the crippling ambiguity and uncertainty which comes from unclear goals.

True accountability is liberating

True accountability is liberating. When you have goal clarity and you are set up for success, you are free to enjoy your autonomy.

Here is how you can use accountability to help you enjoy your autonomy:

1. Be crystal clear about what success looks like

All rookie journalists are taught to answer the 'who, what, where and when' questions in the first paragraph of their report. They are also taught that by far the most interesting question is 'why'. These are the same questions you should be able to answer about any goal you are set, and again by far the most interesting question is 'why'. In the office, you can have an informal and continuing dialogue about this, with greater clarity emerging after each conversation. WFH you have to be far more purposeful and deliberate about achieving this clarity. You need to achieve clarity from the outset to avoid wasted work, time and effort.

For example, your boss asks you to prepare a market analysis for your business. That could mean anything. It could be a one-page SWOT analysis based on existing data or it could be a six-month project combining original customer research, deep competitor analysis and much more. So you have to ask, and keep on asking, the same questions:

- Who wants this?
- Why do they want it?
- When do they need it by?
- Why do they need it by then?
- What will they use it for?
- What are they expecting to see covered in the analysis?
- What is the problem they are trying to solve?

These questions are all about giving you the context so that you can fully understand what you have to deliver. The questions may seem irritating, but they are vital. If you don't ask your boss these questions, you will find yourself asking yourself these same questions. The uncertainty and lack of clarity will be debilitating.

2. Set yourself up for success

Professionals do not like to let anyone down, let alone their boss. That is a curse as much as a blessing. It means that professionals do not like to say 'no' to requests from the boss, even if they are unreasonable. But there is no point in taking on a project unless you are set up for success. Taking on an unreasonable project on a tight deadline with inadequate resources and too many other competing priorities is a recipe for stress and burnout. It is far better to have a difficult conversation about expectations at the start, rather than an impossible conversation about missed goals at the end.

The way to have the difficult conversation about expectations is to be explicit about it: 'Let's see how we can set this assignment up for success'. If you have a boss who does not want to do this, find another boss. This focus on success allows you to ask all the difficult questions:

- How much time and resource will this really take (more than your boss thought, probably)?
- How does this fit with my other priorities (will the boss let you deprioritize other commitments)?
- Who else do we need on board (more resources for you, and you may need your boss to give you political support)?

These questions test the commitment of your boss. If your boss is not prepared to put in the required resources and support, that is a sure signal that it is not a real priority. That leads you to circle back to the discussion about what outcomes are really required. You have to make sure that your goals are in balance with your capacity and capability. If you are in the office, it is easy to have this conversation by walking across to your boss. Working remotely, if you do not do it deliberately and purposefully it will not happen. A scheduled Zoom call makes this conversation far more formal and so the framing of the conversation matters.

Look forward with hope and look backwards with pride

If you frame it as 'setting the project up for success' you make it a positive call.

If you can manage the autonomy and accountability balance well, you will find it empowering and motivating. Good accountability means you can look forward with hope and look backwards with pride at your achievements. Do not shy from accountability: lean into it.

If you are the boss, the same rules apply in reverse:

1. Be crystal clear about what success looks like

Answer the 'who, what, where and when' questions crisply. Have a thorough discussion about the most interesting question: 'why'. Your objective should be to remove all uncertainty and ambiguity about what you need. Be prepared to return to the conversation several times, which is what you would do in the office. Alternatively, if you really want to demotivate your team, a sure way to do so is to be unclear about what you want, communicate it badly and then change your mind. This will ensure your team wastes huge amounts of time and work, and they will be stressed by the ambiguity and uncertainty they face.

2. Set your team member up for success

It is not enough to ask if they have everything they need to succeed. They may well say 'yes' either to please you or because they have not had time to think about it properly. You need to anticipate their needs. The obvious needs are time and budget. Less obvious needs include:

- Access to decision makers.
- Political support in dealing with disruptors and competing agendas.
- Resolving work priorities and workloads for your team.

Don't assume that your team member is happy with, or even aware of, these challenges. If the assignment goes wrong, do not blame your team: look in the mirror. Your role is to ensure that the project is set up for success.

Making the most of autonomy and accountability requires other habits and hacks which are covered more completely elsewhere:

- Pacing your day to sustain your energy and peak performance (Chapter 4).
- Picking the right projects (Chapter 3).
- Delegating effectively as a boss (Chapter 1).

The arrow of autonomy and accountability is flying in one direction only: towards ever-greater autonomy and accountability. The change is being forced by education and the rise of the professional workforce. Flat organizations are a symptom of this change and WFH simply accelerates it. If you want to enjoy the increased autonomy of the future, you have to learn to make the most of the increased accountability that comes with it. With great freedom comes great responsibility: you cannot have one without the other. Make the most of it.

With great freedom comes great responsibility

3.3.4 Mastery for motivation

Mastery is a must-have if you want to stay motivated. You cannot stay motivated if you do not have the skills to do your job well. Hybrid working is both an opportunity and a threat on the path to mastery. To understand this paradox, we have to understand the nature of mastery. To succeed at work, you have to master two sorts of skills and knowledge:

1. *Explicit knowledge.* These are 'know-what' skills which can be readily learned through formal courses, books

and training. Explicit knowledge will include things like finance, accounting and coding.

2. *Tacit knowledge.* These are 'know-how' skills which are much harder to learn from books and courses. These skills might include influencing and persuading people, dealing with crises and setbacks, managing the politics and conflict of an organization.

When you start your career you probably focus on building mastery in explicit knowledge: you learn about the law or programming or accounting. These technical skills are the foundations of your career and will shape how you see the world. But over time, these technical skills become less important to you. You would not expect to see the CEO of a large organization doing the stock check for an audit, even if she had started her career as an accountant. As your career progresses, tacit skills become ever more important. You have to learn to manage the people and politics of the firm. People who focus purely on their technical skills are highly valuable, but will stay in technical roles and not in line management. Most professional careers require a switch of focus from acquiring explicit knowledge to acquiring tacit knowledge over time.

Working remotely gives you the chance to accelerate your explicit knowledge learning, but makes it very hard to build your tacit knowledge. Since tacit knowledge is the key to your career progression, this matters.

In this section we will look at how you can accelerate your path to mastery of both explicit and tacit knowledge and skills. This matters for your career and your motivation. A greater skills base enables you to take on more challenging and more fulfilling roles, and to be more confident of accomplishing them.

1. Mastering explicit knowledge

Most firms and executives are very happy to invest in explicit knowledge. Going on a course to learn about financial strategy is seen as a sign of strength: you are being prepared for a bigger role in the future. And there is no shame in admitting that you are not an expert in all aspects of accounting, unless you are an accountant. The five challenges with this sort of training are:

- Finding the fit between what you need now and what the firm wants is hard. You cannot always get what you want.
- The quality of training is variable: some are life changing and some can be death by PowerPoint. Worst is when you sit in a room having to guess what a facilitator with a franchised theory wants you to write on a flipchart.
- There is often a gap between theory and reality. You do not always get the chance to deploy your newfound knowledge in time to test it and embed it in your personal tool kit.
- Whenever there is a budget crisis, training tends to be one of the budget items that is squeezed first.
- Training is easily squeezed out of the diary by other urgent operational priorities.

WFH gives you the opportunity to resolve all these problems.

- WFH means that you can identify and choose the course you need. You are not limited by what your firm can provide. You can access what you want from anywhere in the world.

- WFH means you are no longer constrained by the approved trainer list of your firm, which may be limited by who is available in the region. You can seek out the best in class solutions from around the world.
- You can do the training on a just-in-time basis: learn what you need, when you need it and then put it straight into action. If there is anything that you do not understand or does not work for you, you can refresh your knowledge immediately online.
- Even if the firm slashes its training budget, many of the best courses are available online for free, or for a very modest monthly subscription.
- WFH lets you manage your time and your priorities. Training online may take up precious free time, but at least it does not get cancelled completely.

The autonomy of WFH allows you to control your destiny and get the sort of training you want, when you want it from the providers you want to use.

The autonomy of WFH allows you to control your destiny

2. Acquiring tacit knowledge

WFH works for acquiring explicit knowledge, but it does not work for acquiring tacit knowledge. To understand this challenge, think about how you have learned your leadership skills and style over the years. When I ask this question of groups, I give them six possible sources of learning about leadership, and let them pick two as their main sources of learning. See which of the following six sources of learning have been most important to you on your leadership journey:

- Books.
- Courses.

- Bosses (good or bad lessons).
- Role models (inside or outside work).
- Colleagues.
- Experience.

The responses are absolutely consistent. Virtually no one picks books or courses, which could be a disaster for an author who runs courses. Many people choose bosses, role models and colleagues, and a forest of hands vote in favour of personal experience. We all learn either from first-hand experience, or from the observed experience of our bosses, colleagues and role models.

This makes sense and is highly practical. Learning from experience means that you learn what works for you in your context. When you see someone do something that works, you try to copy it. If you see someone blow up, you make a quiet note not to make the same mistake. It may not work in theory, but if it works in practice that is all that matters.

There are two problems with this practical approach. The first problem is that it is very slow: it takes years to acquire all the relevant experience to lead a large firm. The second problem is much bigger: learning from experience is a random walk to the future. If you bump into good bosses, role models and experience you learn good lessons and accelerate your career,

Learning from experience is a random walk to the future

whereas poor bosses, role models and experience drive you into a career wilderness. This is where books and courses become relevant. A new graduate cannot read a book and emerge as the complete leader on page 274. But books and courses help you make sense of the nonsense you see and hear and let you take the randomness out of your random walk to the future. They accelerate your path to success: they complement rather than substitute your exploration of the world of tacit knowledge.

Acquiring tacit knowledge through a slow and random walk is not the high road to success. But at least in the office you can join the random walk. In the office you are always seeing and hearing what is working and what is not working. And the famous water cooler is a fine place to discover who is messing up and how they messed up: these are valuable lessons to learn.

WFH makes learning tacit knowledge very hard: you are cut off from observing your colleagues and peers. This matters for everyone at every stage of their career. You need two simple tools to help accelerate acquiring tacit knowledge, tools that will help you craft your own unique success formula which works for you where you work. They are: WWW and EBI.

WWW and EBI are the two questions you should ask yourself after every significant moment in the day, which could be an important Zoom call, or a presentation, or a vital five-minute chat with a senior person in the corridor if you are in the office. They are questions you can ask yourself in a few seconds, and they will help you clarify what works and does not work for you. Here are the two questions:

- WWW: What Worked Well? What did I do right in that event that made it a success? Acquire the fine art of learning from success, because most executives are lousy at learning from success. They assume that success is natural, but success is not natural: it is very hard work. The faster you learn about why you succeed today, the faster you will succeed in future.

- Asking WWW is also vital when things have not gone well. Instead of beating yourself up, take a moment to reflect on what you did to prevent a crisis becoming a disaster. This is very valuable learning which will help you next time you face a crisis.
- EBI: 'Even Better If....' Don't be hard on yourself by asking 'why did I mess up?' because that is negative, depressing and unhelpful. Be more solution focused. Say to yourself: 'It would have been even better if....' Even experienced sales people find this useful. The lessons they learn are usually very simple, such as 'It would have been even better if...I had listened more and talked less...if I had done a bit more research on what they really wanted beforehand....'

WWW and EBI are your secret weapons which let you turbo-charge your acquisition of tacit knowledge. They also help you adapt to new situations, such as WFH and hybrid working, at speed, forcing you to be explicit about what you are observing and learning.

Most executives are lousy at learning from success

WWW and EBI are also highly effective ways of helping your team raise their performance and adapt to new situations. Instil the discipline of making the team reflect on WWW and EBI after every significant team event. Eventually they will become second nature for the team as a whole and for each individual within it. The team becomes a self-improving and agile team. It is essential to ask WWW first. Most post-mortems immediately start with WWW's evil twin: 'What Went Wrong?' but that is a recipe for negativity, the blame game, politics and zero learning. You have to start with the positive 'What Went Well....' If the best thing about a strategy session was the quality of the biscuits, you may have a problem. But normally WWW helps participants reflect positively and discover more good things about the event than they had realized. Asking EBI then forces the team into being solution focused, not problem focused. These are good disciplines for a team to acquire.

3.3.5 Tacit knowledge and the challenge of new joiners

New joiners represent a special challenge in acquiring tacit knowledge. For them, tacit knowledge is about some basic survival skills:

- How do things really get done around here?
- Who can I rely on and who is dangerous?
- Which behaviours are valued and which ones are discouraged?
- How much risk should I take?
- How can I handle my boss?
- Which projects and assignments are the death star projects and how can I avoid them?

The staff handbook will not answer any of these questions. In the office, the new joiner can pick up the answers quickly but WFH they are left to figure it out for themselves. Unless they are mind readers, they will find it hard to work out the real rules of the game.

The obvious and sensible solution is to arrange for new joiners to be based mainly in the office, where they can build this tacit knowledge fast. They will pick up the values of the firm not from reading the firm's values statement, but by working in the firm. But this solution only works if more experienced team members are in the office at the same time. If the experienced team members are all enjoying WFH, then the firm will have an apartheid work force: new joiners in the office and old lags at home, and two different cultures will slowly emerge.

If established team members experience some ambiguity and anxiety when WFH, then you can be sure that new joiners will experience far more anxiety and ambiguity. They do not know what established team members take for granted:

- They do not have the relationships to rely on.
- They do not know the rules of the game.
- They do not know how to get things done.
- They do not know what they are expected to achieve.

Assimilating into the new organization is especially hard where the firm is well established and many staff have spent decades working for the firm: think of government departments, banks and utility companies. These can operate like inward looking clubs. It is hard to gain entry to the club, but once in it is hard to leave. Graduate programmes make the problem worse when WFH: if the graduate has to move function every three months, then she has to find a way of breaking into an established club four times a year without ever going into the club in person. Best practices for helping new joiners land successfully include:

- Have a structured induction programme which enables the new joiner to meet everyone virtually or in person as soon as possible.
- Give each new joiner a welcome package at home and at work, so that they are 100 per cent equipped to be fully functioning from day one. Do not make them beg for support and feel like second-class citizens by not providing them with the tools for the job.
- Ask both the new joiner and their manager to come in on day one: help the joiner meet as many people as possible. Let the joiner see the workplace and get a feel

for what it is like. Complete any admin or mandatory training immediately (health and safety, etc).

- Try to get new joiners to join as a group, and encourage them to socialize. Let them take control and let them support each other.
- When new joiners are in the office, ensure that there is always a critical mass of other team members in the office to help them integrate quickly and effectively.
- Schedule regular formal and informal catch-ups with the new joiner.
- Be crystal clear about goals and expectations and make sure the new joiner is set up for success: this will be an iterative process over many conversations. Remove the ambiguity and anxiety new joiners inevitably feel.

If there is significant WFH, put in place a buddy system with teeth. The buddy needs some basic rules of engagement:

- Conversations between buddy and new joiner must be 100 per cent confidential. The new joiner needs a safe space to ask unsafe questions.
- Check-ins between buddy and new joiner must be regular: at least daily at the start.
- The buddy must be given the time to do the job properly: it cannot be another add-on to an already overloaded priority list.
- The buddy must be willing and able to do the work.
- The success of the integration effort will be part of the year-end appraisal.

All of this is more or less common sense, which is routinely ignored in many firms. A successful new joiner is a massive investment in the future success of the firm: it is worth putting in effort at the start to make the investment worthwhile.

3.4 Key points

1. WFH has led to an epidemic of mental health and motivation challenges.
2. Create the conditions for successful WFH:
   - Set up time boundaries between work and home. Keep work and life separate.
   - Set up a physical workspace that works, and is separate from home space.
   - Create clear routines, with regular breaks in the day. Break between calls.
   - Take exercise.
   - Reach out: a problem shared is a problem halved, a joy shared is a joy doubled.
3. Manage your inner game. Be your best friend, not worst critic, in your internal chatter.
   - Avoid ruminating, catastrophizing and mind reading.
   - Discover the positive side of life: the 'three blessings' exercise.
4. Build your mastery, which is both explicit (know-what skills) and tacit (know-how skills).
   - Use WWW and EBI to build your unique leadership success formula.
5. Motivating people remotely is hard, and impossible by email.
6. Create the conditions in which your team can discover their intrinsic motivation.
   - Relationships: show appreciation of good work; be collaborative on a tit for tat basis.
   - Autonomy and accountability increase when WFH. Make accountability work for you by having high goal clarity and setting yourself up for success before accepting an assignment.

- Mastery: WFH increases your ability to master explicit skills. The office is vital for building context-specific tacit skills.
- Purpose: craft your job so that it has a sense of meaning and purpose to you.

7. Ensure new joiners acquire the values and tacit knowledge to succeed by working in the office, not WFH.

4

Process: fix the plumbing of remote working

In the office, people know how things work and they have the tools for the job. WFH was a giant leap into the unknown. It was a huge experiment in new ways of working. But many firms and teams already had deep experience of remote working, and of working on global teams. Global teams are remote teams on steroids: you cannot see your colleagues, and they may have a different time zone, language and culture. Some firms had to discover the solution, others already knew it.

This chapter summarizes the best practices of remote working and WFH. There is no theory, simply a record of what works. The record is based on original research around the world, across industries and from the smallest to the largest firms. The good news is that there are consistent practices which help WFH work.

This chapter covers the practicalities of making remote working function properly:

1. *Set yourself up for success.*
2. *Set your team up for success.*
3. *Create the rhythms and routines of success.*
4. *Create your team's own unique success formula.*

5. *Collaborate remotely: presentations, workshops and conferences.*

6. *Make meetings work.*

These are rational problems to which there are clear and rational solutions. Fixing the plumbing may be unglamorous, but it is vital infrastructure for personal and team success.

4.1 Set yourself up for success

Some people love WFH, some hate it. But love it or hate it, WFH is here to stay. Globally, staff consistently express a preference for a hybrid model of working: part of the week in the office and part at home. Even in Japan, where homes are really not set up for WFH, hybrid working is now in demand. Perhaps the joy of commuting three or four hours every day wears off after 20 years. There are clear benefits to WFH: less commuting; more flexible working hours; less distraction than at work; potentially better work-life balance. But WFH can also be a poisoned chalice: stress, overwork and loss of work-life balance.

To make the most of WFH, fix the plumbing in four areas:

- Establish boundaries between work and life.
- Create the rhythms and routines of success.
- Manage your energy levels.
- Ensure you have the right tools for the job.

4.1.1 Establish boundaries between work and life

In the past, when you left the office you left work. But in the new world, you may never leave work; it is with you all the time at home. This leads to increasing levels of stress, burnout and demotivation. You have to regain control of your life. Do not let the office take over you and your home. You can do this by recreating the boundaries that occur naturally when you work from the office.

Commuters who hated commuting are discovering that there was value to the commute. It created a transition and a boundary between work and home. The hard working executive could slowly unwind and become the loving parent or spouse by the **In the new world, you may never leave work** time they reached home. Equally, the transition from home to work gave time to prepare mentally for the day, rehearse key conversations and order priorities. Even Superman needed time to transition, in a phone box, from a mild journalist to world-saving hero. And part of the transition was to put on a different set of clothes: wearing underpants outside your tights may work on Zoom and in the movies but is not necessarily best practice.

Section 3.1 emphasized the need to look after yourself so that you can look after others. You have to recreate the home-work boundaries that occur naturally when you work in an office. Some of the simple hacks include:

- *Leave your house to go for a short walk*, perhaps to buy a coffee from a local shop and then come back. Mentally, you are leaving your house and when you come back you are arriving at your office. You will have recreated your commute in a way that is probably far more congenial than your regular commute.
- *Change clothes.* Don't work in your pyjamas, because then work and life becomes hopelessly entangled. Some people even put on a suit or regular work clothes for when they are working. This creates a clear boundary between work and home.

- *Create a separate workspace*: your home office. If you are lucky, this might be a separate room but at least find a separate space. One interviewee for this book was forced to work from her own bedroom in a shared flat. To make an intolerable situation more tolerable she had a ritual of laying out a rug on her bed when she started work. This created a minimal boundary between work and life: when the rug was out, she worked. When she finished work, the rug and laptop disappeared and she could resume social life.

Boundaries are vital for both productivity and wellbeing. When you are at work, work without distraction. When you leave

Boundaries are vital for both productivity and wellbeing

work, relax without worrying about work. When home and work co-mingle you can be distracted at work and worry at home so clear boundaries help.

4.1.2 Create the rhythms and routines of success

Many organizations are reporting a WFH productivity miracle. This is not because staff have become more productive per working hour, it is because they are working far longer hours. This is sustainable during a crisis, but it is not a sustainable way of working long term. The sustainable solution is not to work longer, but to work smarter. Achieving more in less time is the holy grail of productivity. Fortunately, you can do this if you can stay focused when you need to be focused.

The three killers of productivity are interruptions, distractions and delay. These are deadly in both the office and at home. The good news is that the productivity bar is remarkably low. The US Bureau of Labor Statistics did a survey of over 20,000 office workers to find out how many productive working hours they delivered every day. Heroically, the Department counted meeting time as productive time, which will come as a surprise to many office workers. They found that on average, workers were productive for 2 hours and 58 minutes every day. The rest of the day was lost to:

- Interruptions from colleagues.
- Distractions such as social media, online shopping and following the news.
- Taking rest breaks, going to the water cooler or grabbing coffee or lunch.

Interruptions were found to be especially damaging. A separate study of coders found that after each interruption, it would take the coder 15 minutes to get back up to speed and that their work was more error prone. All it takes is for two colleagues per hour to swing by and say hello,

The three killers of productivity are interruptions, distractions and delay

offer a coffee or discuss the latest video game, and that is half the day lost to trivial interruptions.

Working from home you will not suffer all the interruptions and distractions of office life; instead, you will suffer all the interruptions and distractions of home life. These can be especially acute if you are looking after children, home schooling or you have other care responsibilities, but unlike work, you are better able to control the interruptions and distractions at home.

Here is the schedule of one executive and working mother:

- 7–8am: catch up on admin, emails, prepare the day.
- 8–9.30am: family time and go to school time.
- 9.30am–3pm: core work time, especially for meetings. Time off for lunch break.

- 3–6.30pm back from school, family time.
- 6.30–8pm work time, for solo activities: writing and reviewing reports etc.
- After 8pm: me time. Gym, relaxing etc.

Inevitably, virtually no day works out as planned. But at least she has a structure she can flex: she is in control of events rather than being controlled by events. It is also a smart way of differentiating between the sorts of work she needs to do. Core hours are her interactive hours, and other hours are for when she needs to do solo work.

Your rhythms and routines will doubtless be different. What matters is that you create routines that work for you. The office forced routines on you; WFH gives you the freedom to create your own routines, but make sure you have a routine. If you have no routine, you will struggle with overwork and stress. Once you have a structure to your day, you can still flex it when you need to.

4.1.3 Manage your energy levels

An executive with a full diary must be very busy and productive, mustn't she?

She will clearly be very busy, because the diary proves that; whether she's productive and effective is more questionable. Endless studies show that it is very hard to sustain physical or mental effort for very long: you might sprint for 10 seconds, you cannot sprint for an hour. And in the office, there is a cruel and unusual form of punishment called death by PowerPoint: after an hour of listening to a presentation, most people lose the will to live.

The need for rest breaks was discovered over 100 years ago by the patron saint of Time and Motion: FW Taylor. He spent his life figuring out how to maximize the output of workers. He was 100 per cent on the side of management and his methods were always controversial. They were captured by Charlie Chaplin in the film *Modern Times*: he got caught up in a machine that forced him to work faster and faster. So it may be a surprise to find that FW Taylor insisted that all workers rested for at least five minutes each hour, even if they did not feel tired. He was not doing it to be kind to the workers; he was doing it because he discovered that short rests maximize productivity in the long run.

As with physical work, so with mental work: rest breaks are not a sign of weakness, they are key to sustaining productivity. If a colleague turned up to work drunk, they would probably be fired on the spot, whereas if another colleague was still in the office when you arrived in the morning, after an all-night shift, you might praise them for their effort. But in practice, the work of the tired hero and the drunk will be similar. A Stanford University test compared the reaction times of 113 marginally sleep deprived individuals with the reaction times of 80 other individuals who had slept well. Reaction times of the sleep deprived were 20 per cent worse than the others. The good sleepers were then helped to get increasingly drunk (all in the name of science, of course). The good sleepers, even after they were legally drunk for the purposes of driving, still had better reaction times than the poor sleepers who were stone cold sober. It appears you really can sleep your way to success.

In the office, rest breaks occur naturally between meetings. You normally have a few minutes to walk between meetings, to grab a coffee, have a quick chat with a colleague in the corridor or go to the rest room. WFH, these natural breaks disappear as the tyranny of scheduled video meetings takes over. It is technically easy to switch immediately at the top of each hour from one meeting to the next. FW Taylor would be dismayed: you are denying yourself the vital five

Rest breaks are not a sign of weakness

minutes' recovery time to help yourself be more productive in the next hour.

Here are two ways you can structure quick rest breaks into your day to make it more productive:

- *Schedule meetings to be 25 minutes or 50 minutes long.* This gives the crucial mini-break between meetings to rest, decompress from the last meeting and prepare for the next meeting. In practice, you will find that the time discipline forces everyone on the call to be more focused. You have a better meeting and you build in a rest break.
- *Use short interval scheduling.* This is a simple practice of breaking large tasks into small pieces, and then giving yourself a time limit for completing the small piece. For instance, writing a training manual is a huge task. But in practice, the manual will be composed of many small elements. Focus on writing just one of these elements in the next 45 minutes, or even just half of it. Convert the marathon of writing the training manual into a series of short sprints with rest breaks in between. Once you have completed each element of the task, reward yourself with a trip to the coffee machine, or take a moment to look at social media.

There are many variations of short interval scheduling. A popular variant is the Pomodoro technique, named after a very kitsch Pomodoro kitchen timer from the 1980s. It looked like a tomato (*pomodoro*, in Italian). Set the timer, traditionally to 25 minutes, and then focus 100 per cent on the task in hand, permitting no interruptions. Then give yourself a short break. Repeat four times and then give yourself a longer break of 15–30 minutes. Some people find this helps concentration, others find having their day ruled by a kitsch kitchen timer to be distracting. Use what works for you, from a smart watch to an hourglass timer, to help you convert your day into a series of focused sprints.

The common features of these productivity techniques are:

- Break large tasks into small pieces which can be achieved in 25 or 50 minutes.
- Focus on one task at a time in each 25 to 50 minute block of time.
- Avoid interruptions.
- Give yourself a break at the end of each period.
- Repeat.

4.1.4 *Ensure you have the right tools for the job*

How many hours will you spend working from home over a career? Even if you only do 600 hours a year, over 40 years that comes to 24,000 hours you will spend working from home. It pays to make sure you are set up the right way.

Let's start with the chair you are sitting in at home. Many people do not want to overpay for a chair but that is a false economy. If you are going to spend 24,000 hours sitting in a chair, it pays to get a good chair. If your employer does not provide you with a good chair, they may be courting litigation as staff slowly succumb to endless back problems. But rather than wait to acquire a back problem and a court case, invest in a good chair yourself. The good news is that there is a vigorous market in excellent second-hand office chairs, if you cannot afford a new one.

It pays to make sure you are set up the right way

Your physical work environment at home should be as good as your physical environment in the office. In most countries, employers have the same health and safety responsibilities for staff working from home as they do for staff working at the office. The temporary hacks staff used to work and survive during the pandemic often fell far short of what is acceptable long term. When you sit down to work, you should look like this:

- Shoulders relaxed.
- Wrists straight (level with desk).
- Back supported.
- Feet supported.
- Head level: eyes level with top of screen.
- Screen about arm's length from eyes.

Working on laptops leads to the familiar sight of people crouching over their computer, which is not good for their backs. If you are going to spend hours with a laptop then put it on a box so that you can look at it with your head level. This will require using a separate keyboard at desk level. This is a modest expense and a good long-term investment.

Having the right technology matters. A poor internet connection is inexcusable. In the office it would be unacceptable to keep on dropping in and out of a meeting; it is equally unacceptable to drop in and out of video meetings because of technical problems. Your employer should ensure you have good internet connections at home and work and should pay for it: they would not expect you to pay for your internet connection at work.

Beyond the internet, there are raging arguments about what are the right office productivity tools for remote and hybrid teams. Each platform has its evangelists who will swear that they have found the very best and futureproof technology solution. In practice, the technology is always changing and evolving. IT should stand for Intermediate Technology because it keeps on progressing. You do not need to find the world's best technology solution; you need to find the same solution as the rest of your team and firm, so that you can work seamlessly with them.

The challenge comes when you work with an external stakeholder who may well have different technology solutions. Most of the time these differences do not matter, but they do matter if you have an important conference involving new partners. Set up a technical rehearsal a day before to make sure you understand how their technology works, so that you do not spend half the actual meeting getting distracted by technical challenges about how to set up chat groups, break outs, deal with logins, screen sharing and all the other basics which either make a conference look professional or unprofessional.

4.2 Set your team up for success

The heroic leader is past their sell-by date. As a leader, you cannot succeed alone: you have to succeed with your team. That means that you have to set your team up for success both at home and at the office. The way you do this is different from before the COVID-19 pandemic but the challenges are similar to the personal challenges of setting up success:

- Establish boundaries between work and life.
- Manage energy levels: avoid burnout.
- Focus on goals not presence.
- Ensure your team has the tools to WFH.
- Design the office to suit the nature of your work.

4.2.1 Establish boundaries between work and life
Employers were baffled by the pandemic. Several reported that workloads did not increase, once staff had adjusted to the initial crisis but despite that, staff reported increased workloads, stress and burnout. There were two problems:

- Staff lost boundaries between home and office: mentally, they never left the office.
- Uncertainty over goals and over their job security led to over-delivery and overwork.

Your team cannot set boundaries to their work if you do not set boundaries for their work. You need to set boundaries in terms of both time and workload/goals.

Time-based boundaries are about agreeing when work should happen. For office-based teams, this is obvious: work should happen when they are in the office. This gives clear structure, but it is also a rigid structure that does not help people who need flexible working hours, such as parents and carers.

The heroic leader is past their sell-by date

WFH gives you the chance to create far more flexible boundaries that will help the team; the risk is that you create no boundaries, which will eventually destroy the team.

We have already seen the case of the working mother who developed a WFH schedule that meant that her actual working hours were:

- 7–8am: catch up on admin, emails, prepare the day.
- 9.30am–3pm: core work time, especially for meetings. Time off for lunch break.
- 6.30–8pm work time, for solo activities: writing and reviewing reports etc.

This schedule only works if the team leader helps it work. It requires that the whole team agrees on core hours when they are available for meetings and calls: in this case the core hours would be 9.30am to 3pm. Enforcing these hours means enforcing a 'no meetings' rule after 3pm. This may seem idle and an irresponsible waste of time, but it is not. Core hours allow for four and a half hours of meeting time every day, allowing time off for lunch. If your team is meeting longer than that every day, you probably have a productivity problem. Making boundaries work requires discipline and focus about what happens when.

These boundaries collapse in the face of instant communications, which demand instant responses. You need to agree expectations on when communications need a reply. The danger with the always-on messaging services is that we all feel the need to be always-on as well. Answering messages at 3am shows dedication, but is a quick way to burnout. Setting boundaries on responding to communications leads to an inevitable objection: what if there is something really urgent which needs an instant reply? The answer is very old fashioned: pick up the phone. If your message is genuinely urgent, you should feel you can phone your colleague at 3am and demand an instant reply. Being faced with the prospect of explaining to a colleague why you have woken her at 3am is a quick way to discover whether your request really is that urgent. Leaving a text/email/instant message is a good way of inducing guilt while avoiding taking responsibility for being anti-social.

The right boundaries are different for each team. They depend on the needs of the team and the needs of the work, and they will vary over time. You have to agree these boundaries with your team and every team member needs to buy into and respect the boundaries.

Making boundaries work requires discipline

As with all boundaries, there is a danger that boundaries can become a prison, not a framework. If you stick rigidly to the boundaries 100 per cent of the time and never change them, they become a prison which inhibits the work of your team. You need some flexibility, especially to cope with peaks of work and short deadlines. As a team leader you should be able to predict when these peaks and crunch deadlines are coming and you can then set expectations with the team about the need to change hours or work longer hours. Most team members understand this and will be happy to do it, provided they are given enough notice in advance. This allows people to change personal events or re-arrange childcare as necessary. If you want to annoy your team, a sure way to do it is to impose changes at the last moment which will cause maximum disruption to your team's lives. That sort of chaos is normally the sign of an ineffective team leader who is unable to predict and manage workloads well; it is sometimes the sign of a team leader who does not care about the team. Either way, it leads to loss of respect and trust from the team, and makes recruiting the best talent to your team harder in future.

If you manage work boundaries well, you are in danger of becoming the sort of boss people want to work for, as opposed to the sort of boss people have to work for. Effective and flexible boundaries, combined with hybrid working, also allows you to recruit from a wider talent pool. It lets you recruit the talent that needs more flexible hours to deal with caring responsibilities at home. Good boundaries are good for you, for your team, for performance, for recruiting and for diversity.

4.2.2 Manage energy levels: avoid burnout

Do not expect your team to give 100 per cent for eight hours a day. FW Taylor studied labourers moving pigs of iron at a steel mill. He found that by giving workers a five-minute break every hour, he could raise their productivity dramatically. Labourers went from moving 12 tonnes of iron per shift to moving 47 tonnes of iron per shift (with other improvements such as redesigned shovels). Your challenge is to ensure that your team can shift the office equivalent of 47 tonnes of work, not 12 tonnes of work. Short rests are vital.

Two simple hacks help manage energy over the day.

1. Schedule meetings for 25 minutes and 50 minutes, not 30 minutes and 60 minutes. We have encountered this hack already. It gives everyone a few vital minutes of decompression time between meetings. If 50-minute meetings force people to be less long-winded and to stay focused, that is not necessarily a bad thing.

2. Break up the routine. Not every WFH meeting has to be a video meeting. If everyone is tethered to their desk all day, staring at a screen, they will burn out as the day goes on. There is a very effective alternative technology that you can use: the telephone. For a one-to-one call, suggest that you both use the phone and go for a walk. This breaks the routine, gives you some fresh air and often leads to far better conversations. When people are relaxed, they often think better, they are less likely to be on guard and as a result the call is likely to be shorter and to the point. Do not try this hack in a blizzard.

The problem of routine is acute for people WFH. At least in the office, there is constant variety: interruptions, trips to the coffee machine, a short walk across the office to talk to a colleague, a change of scenery as you walk to a meeting. At home, it is easy to become tethered to a desk and a screen all day. In theory, the lack of interruptions should help productivity but in practice, people need breaks to their routine to sustain energy and concentration levels.

Not every WFH meeting has to be a video meeting

In Uganda, large meetings regularly include an energizer exercise. One person will lead the team in a 30-second fun exercise which might be a chant or a dance of some sort. Everyone seems to have a store of simple fun exercises to share. When COVID-19 forced people to work online, they simply continued these energizers online. They are a wonderful way of breaking routine, building the team and raising energy levels. You may or may not like the idea of energizers for your team, but with creativity you can find other ways of helping your team break the routine and sustain energy for the whole day.

4.2.3 Focus on goals, not presence

In the office there is a dangerous assumption that presence = productivity. In a world of ambiguous work where productivity is a team effort, it can take quite a long time to find out who is genuinely productive and who simply talks a good game.

WFH makes it harder to prove that you are being productive. This helps explain why many team members have felt more stress when WFH: they feel under constant pressure to show that they are being productive, because the presence = productivity formula no longer applies.

As team leader you can reduce team stress and increase team productivity by being very clear about what needs to be done and when. We have already seen in Chapter 2 that goal setting, far from being Management 101, is especially hard on hybrid teams. In the office, you can rely on an iterative process of clarifying and checking on goals and progress. This is informal, quick and effective. When your team is remote you have to be more purposeful and deliberate in setting goals, clarifying them and checking on progress.

Clarity does not come from writing goals down, because you can never capture everything that is relevant. There will always be:

• Questions of clarification.
• Unintentional misunderstandings.

- Questions to understand context: knowing the 'why' of a goal is often as important as knowing the 'what'.
- Requests for support, resources and help in dealing with blockages.
- Suggestions for better ways of going about things and fine-tuning the goal.

It is through this process of discussion that your team member can build ownership and commitment to delivering the goal. Once they understand the context, have shaped the goal to be deliverable and have the support they need, they will start to own the goal. You cannot achieve this by writing the goal down and sending it in a message to your team member.

Once you and your team have total goal clarity you achieve three outcomes:

- Enhanced productivity, not enhanced presence.
- Greater accountability: you know who does what.
- Less team stress. Clear goals create clear boundaries around expectations.

Achieving goal clarity demands patience and persistence. It is very easy to become frustrated when a team member does not immediately understand what you want. Unfortunately, most team members are not mind readers. It takes time for them to fully understand what you want. In the office, this understanding builds informally in a series of conversations which may last a few seconds or a few minutes, but WFH you should expect to have repeated conversations about goals and targets. WFH team members' anxiety will rise dramatically if they feel they do not fully understand what is required. They

Most team members are not mind readers

will fear that they are wasting their time on work that is not 100 per cent on track.

4.2.4 Ensure your team has the tools to WFH
In the office you have a legal obligation to ensure your staff work in an environment that is healthy and safe, both physically and mentally. You have exactly the same obligation wherever they work, including at home. In the office, you may have occupational health experts to advise you on best practice but these best practices can disappear completely when people work from home. That is not just bad for productivity: it is also storing up potential future litigation.

The right tools are not just about technology. You have to help team members have a home office that works: a good chair, desk, computer stand and possibly noise-cancelling headphones. Some team members may be unable to WFH: find alternative co-working spaces nearby where they can work instead. You would not expect anyone in the office to perch on the end of a bed to work, and you should not expect them to have to do that at home either.

4.2.5 Design the office to suit the nature of your work
In the last 20 years, offices evolved in only one direction: cram more people in. Average space per office worker in London decreased from 22 square metres to 10 square metres over this period. The logic was that open plan working fostered greater learning and collaboration but in practice, these were good excuses for reducing the rent bill. Hot desking was simply a continuation of the same trend of saving on space and rent.

Not surprisingly, staff became disenchanted with office life. Hot desking and the battery hen approach to office staffing had real problems:

- It was hard to concentrate with the constant background noise.

- There were endless interruptions.
- You were under constant surveillance by peers and bosses.
- There was nowhere to have confidential conversations.
- You had no space to call your own, no space to personalize.

Despite these drawbacks, many staff started to discover the joys of the office when they could no longer go to it; you only know what matters when you no longer have it. WFH meant that we are in danger of falling in love with the office again, despite its many drawbacks. We discovered that the office is a highly effective machine for some sorts of work. It is very good for:

- Collaboration, creativity and problem solving.
- Learning, especially for new hires who can pick up how things work, at speed.
- Communication: miscommunications are easy to spot and to fix in real time.
- Workload management: it is easy to see who is struggling and who is coasting.
- Social networks and trust building.
- Creating structure by separating work and life.
- Idea generation through serendipitous conversations by the water cooler.
- Influencing key decisions and people by 'accidentally' bumping into the right person in the corridor before and after meetings.

WFH has helped us discover the value of the much-maligned office. WFH also revealed a universal truth: not all work is created equal. Some work is ideally suited to being in the office; some work is ideally suited to WFH. This gives you the chance to reconfigure the office around the way work happens, not around the quarterly rent bill. In practice, there are three different sorts of work in the office which need three different sorts of space:

The office is a highly effective machine for some sorts of work

- Meeting zones for formal meetings, from small to large.
- Quiet zones where staff need no interruptions or phone calls to do high concentration work.
- Collaborative zones where staff interruptions are part of the traditional role of the office: encouraging communication, collaboration, learning, networking and informal decision making and problem solving.

During the day, staff will move between all three modes of work and need all three types of working spaces. Where an office is designed around the needs of the work and the team, there is a danger that staff may fall back in love with the office. They may even discover the knack of delivering the office equivalent of 47 tonnes of pig iron, not 12 tonnes. It is time to make the office work for you instead of you working for the office.

At a corporate level, firms are discovering that these three sorts of workspace mean that they do not need as much space as they used to, even after they allow for plenty of space for meeting and entertaining clients. The race is on to offload or sublet space and to save money. The danger is that saving money becomes the goal of the exercise, rather than a by-product of the exercise. The correct starting point is to understand how to make the

The challenge is to make the office of the future better, not just cheaper

office work best, not how to reduce costs most. Smart employers will make their offices smaller but more attractive, so that staff want to come in. The lure of cost savings will ensure that hybrid working becomes standard practice in future. The challenge is to make the office of the future better, not just cheaper.

4.3 Create the rhythms and routines of success

The office is a wonderful communications machine. A huge amount of vital information flows rapidly and informally across the office every day. This makes it relatively easy to:

- Manage workloads.
- Monitor performance.
- Assess morale.
- Identify and deal with blockages.
- Set goals.
- Discuss priorities.
- Collaborate.
- Influence decisions.

In the office, all these things happen naturally over the course of the day as you bump into colleagues. All of this can also be done remotely, but you have to be far more purposeful and deliberate about all these activities. This means you need to create a series of rhythms and routines to replicate what happens in the office.

If you do not have clear routines for dealing with all these communication challenges, you will drown in communication. Excess communication is a curse for many remote teams: teams can spend the whole time communicating and no time doing.

Just as the office needs different spaces for different sorts of work, so the team needs to do different sorts of work at different times of day. In the office, you can design physical boundaries; remotely, you can design time-based boundaries. The key boundary to build is between collaborative work and solo work: if half the team is trying to collaborate and the other half is trying to do solo work, you have chaos.

Where you draw the boundary depends on the sort of work you do. Lawyers reviewing contracts and case material will need a large amount of solo time, as will IT coders. That is high concentration work best done alone. In contrast, creative types in an advertising agency will be heavily skewed towards collaborative time.

Whatever sort of work you do, perhaps the single most powerful communication tool you have at your disposal is the morning YTH meeting, which can be virtual or in person. In a YTH meeting each team member has 90 seconds (or two minutes) to tell the rest of the team three things:

- Y: what I did Yesterday.
- T: what I will do Today.
- H: where I need Help or support to deal with blockages.

In one short meeting you achieve several goals:

- Every team member knows who is doing what, and they understand where their work fits in.
- You can monitor progress overall.
- You can hold team members to account: have they been able to achieve what they said they would achieve?
- You can identify problems early, and can help resolve them over the balance of the day.

- The whole team starts the day focused and purposefully.
- You can probably see who is struggling personally and you can follow up with them.

The brevity of the meeting matters. If you allow people to talk at length, they can hide by distracting attention from what matters with lots of unnecessary detail. It is far harder to hide in a short report. Brevity forces clarity, on what you have done, **Brevity forces clarity** what you will do and where you need help.

For the rest of the day, you have to agree with your team which routines work best for them. A useful way of thinking about this is to split time into three distinct zones when the team should:

1. Be on a call together (for instance, for the YTH meeting).
2. Have a Zoom-free zone, for solo work.
3. Be available for calls if required.

Doing this will also help define core working hours. WFH should allow for far more flexible working patterns. Working parents may well find that they do their solo work after children have gone to bed. They may work late, but they need time off from the middle of the afternoon for childcare. That may force core working hours to be from 9.30am to 3pm, with a YTH call starting the formal day at 9.30am.

If you want team members to have time when they can really focus on solo work, you also need to set expectations about when emails and instant messaging should expect replies. There is little point in creating a Zoom-free zone if team members are spending all their time on email, Slack and other instant messaging platforms. Be clear about what sort of work happens when. You do not have to stick rigidly to this, day after day and month after month because workloads and work patterns change from time to time. Your daily YTH meeting is a chance to change the rules of the game for the day. If there is a day when you need intense collaboration across the whole team, you can ditch the Zoom-free zone completely, for instance.

4.4 Create your team's own unique success formula

- Q1: what is the nature of successful hybrid team work?
- Q2: what is the nature of successful work?
- Q3: what is the nature of success?

There is no universal success formula, for anything – or if there is such a formula, someone is hiding it very well. Your team will be unique because of the work you do and the team you have, and that means you have to work out your own unique success formula for hybrid working. The principles laid out in this book give you the basics of what works. How you apply the principles to your team will be unique to your team.

Fortunately, there is a method for creating your own success formula. It is called a Methods Adoption Workshop. This is a grand title for a simple meeting, where you gather your team to agree what the rules of engagement will be for your team.

Work out your own unique success formula

The workshop achieves two goals at the same time.

- It helps the whole team agree how they will work together.
- It is a highly effective team building tool, because everyone gets to know each other and gets to have some ownership over their destiny.

The Methods Adoption Workshop has three steps:

- *Step 1: Brainstorm/agree the rules of engagement.*
- *Step 2: Stress test your answers.*
- *Step 3: Review your progress and solutions after one month.*

Here is how each step works:

Step 1: Brainstorm/agree the rules of engagement
Topics you should cover, which you can vary to suit the needs of your team:

1. Perform initial introductions, team building exercise and context setting.
   a. Agree the desired outcomes for the day.
2. Agree the rhythms of the week:
   a. When shall we be in the office and when shall we be out?
3. Agree the rhythms and routines of the day:
   a. What are the core working hours?
   b. Do we start the day with a YTH meeting?
   c. Do we have any Zoom-free zones during the day?
   d. When should we expect answers to emails/instant messages?
4. Agree what the infrastructure will be:
   a. What technology platforms will we use for communications and collaboration?
   b. What support is needed to set up remote working spaces?
   c. What will our office space look like? Will we have dedicated or shared space? How will that work with other teams and their needs?
5. How will we make decisions?
   a. What are the key decisions we need to make as a team?

    b. What are our roles in each decision? Perform a RACI analysis: who is Responsible and Accountable for each decision, who needs to be Consulted and Informed?

    c. How do we deal with disagreements?

6. What will success look like for this team?

    a. What are the deliverables we need to achieve and by when?

7. What is our working culture?

    a. What are the two or three values we hold most dear, and how will we keep each other honest about them?

8. How will we deal with setbacks and problems?

    a. Workload problems, changes of priority from the top.

    b. Political, organizational barriers to success.

    c. Personal stress, welfare and working conditions.

9. Agree the next steps:

    a. How will we record our agreements?

    b. How will we keep ourselves and each other honest about our agreements, and what will we do when someone falls short?

    c. When and how will we review progress and refine our charter?

Step 2: Stress test your answers

The danger with step one is that you come up with worthy intentions that do not survive the first contact with reality. Your stress test is effectively a reality test: how will these proposals work in the messy reality of real life?

For instance, when the *Financial Times* was taken over by the Nikkei, both sides sat down to agree how to work together. One of the principles they agreed was 'editorial independence', which both sides readily agreed was vital. So what does that really mean? They decided to stress test the answer by asking what would happen if there was an incident in the South China Sea, in an area contested by Japan and China. The Nikkei would inevitably carry a pro-Japan slant on events but what if the *FT* decided that they wanted to take a more pro-China stance? Nikkei could, as the owners of the *FT*, dictate a pro-Japan line. They discussed this and agreed editorial independence means editorial independence: the *FT* would be free to pursue whatever line they wanted.

Similarly, the British Council came up with a value around 'professional regard'. What does that mean? They stress tested this by looking at a series of cases where a colleague had done something unexpected, or perhaps not delivered something or made a mistake. These things can happen easily in a global organization, because misunderstandings are very common across time zones, language and culture. In each case they identified that the right response was to assume that the colleague was a valued professional and was doing their best, often in difficult circumstances. That in turn meant that the blame game of 'he said, I said, but she didn't and we meant, but they should have so I couldn't....' is the wrong response. Professional regard means:

- Seeking to understand not to judge.
- Seeking solutions not blame.
- Focusing on action not on analysis.

This was then highlighted with a series of cases to show how professional regard led to positive outcomes. The stress testing should convert theory into a reality that everyone can understand and act on.

Step 3: Review your progress and solutions after one month
However good your initial workshop is, you will find that reality throws up all sorts of unexpected challenges that your

initial Methods Plan does not cope with well. Fortunately, your methods plan is not a Constitution set down by Founding Fathers which cannot be changed for hundreds of years. It is a working, living document to help you day to day.

This review workshop will be shorter than the initial workshop. A simple review format is a critical incident review where you focus on two topics: WWW and EBI. We have met WWW and EBI before as useful learning tools. We can use the same tools to improve the quality of team working through the critical incident review. A critical incident is anything that went particularly well or was a real challenge or was especially important. Review these incidents through the lens of WWW and EBI:

WWW: What Worked Well. It is vital to catch your team succeeding, because this is a success formula they can build on. WWW achieves three things for you:

- Captures valuable learning about what works.
- Builds positive momentum among the team: they can see that they can succeed.
- Creates a valuable habit of constant learning and looking positively at events.

EBI: Even Better If.... When looking at setbacks, negative behaviour can run riot. As a result, many teams avoid looking at setbacks too closely, so they limit their learning to what the rumour mill suggests might have happened. Any review that starts 'you messed up because...' is going to have an ugly ending.

Instead, insist that you look at any setback by starting your comment with: 'It would have been Even Better If....'

This EBI sounds hokey, but it is highly effective because it:

- Avoids the blame game.
- Forces everyone to be solution focused.

- Encourages real learning.
- Makes it easy to be (relatively) open and honest about setbacks.

This review workshop is not just about refining your rules of engagement. It is about helping your team engage in continual learning and it is helping build your group of individuals into a real team.

Steps 3 and beyond: continue to review your charter and your progress on a quarterly basis

This is your chance to convert your team charter into a living document which is relevant and useful. You can use it to continue the process of learning and team building. Continual reviews matter, especially where you have new team members and/or a new set of priorities to deal with.

> **Convert your team charter into a living document which is relevant and useful**

New priorities will inevitably change workloads and work patterns: you will need to adjust your charter to fit the new reality. For a well-established team, this is fairly straightforward. The real challenge comes when the team has to integrate new team members. It can be very hard for a new team member to come into a well-established team, which can have the feeling of anything from a club to a cult with its own culture and belief system, and the challenge is especially acute when the team is largely remote. The new team member is not in the office and cannot see how things really work, who does what, how decisions are made and what matters to whom. And it is more or less impossible to explain all this tacit knowledge, either in a meeting or in a written document. The team charter will not make much sense to a newcomer, because they will have no knowledge of all the case history which turns the charter into a living document.

Quarterly reviews of the team charter give new team members the chance to absorb how things work in practice. As ever, the discovered truth is valued more than the revealed truth. The discovered truth is better understood and has greater ownership than having the truth revealed in a charter or a policy document. The discovery process is inefficient compared to revealing the truth: discussion takes more time than handing over some papers. What the discovery process lacks in efficiency, it makes up for in effectiveness, and it is a good way to help new team members become full members of your team.

4.5 Collaborate remotely: presentations, workshops and conferences

In this section you will discover that you do not need to replicate the physical world of presentations, workshops and conferences online. If you simply try replication, you will conclude that the virtual world is a pale imitation of the real world, but the virtual world is not necessarily better or worse: it is just different. Your challenge is to make the most of those differences. Remote working creates as many opportunities as it creates challenges.

The glass-half-full view of remote conferences is clear:

1. No spontaneous chats with colleagues.
2. Unable to observe body language.
3. Hard to brainstorm in a group remotely.
4. Less socialization, team building and trust building.
5. No time at the bar at your employer's expense.
6. No trip to an exotic location, or hotel conference suite.

The glass-half-full view shows that remote conferences and workshops can be far better:

1. Include more people.
2. Offer wider experiences.
3. Attract the best speakers and experts.
4. Quicker, better, more focused break out groups.
5. Better mixing of participants.
6. Better use of time.
7. Lower cost.

Here is how you can deliver the glass-half-full version of remote conferences:

4.5.1 Include more people

The global NGO, STiR Education, wanted to bring its global funders, government partners and staff together for an annual conference. The physical conference meant that many VIPs could not attend: the long haul travel would take too long for them. The remote conference made it easy for all the key players to attend for the key passages of the conference. It was also a chance for all STiR staff around the world to attend, which would not have been possible with a traditional conference. The remote conference achieved far more, for more people, than the physical conference could have achieved.

The Innovation Unit in New Zealand found that co-creating solutions for elderly citizens was easier online. Co-creation was tricky in the physical world because many of the elderly were immobile and hard to reach. By moving online, they could include the elderly easily in their co-creation. They were included at the time and place that suited them, for as long as they needed. Increasingly, technology is finding solutions to help replicate the flip chart and Post-It note experience. These collaboration tools (Miro, for instance) are useful; they take some getting used to but they will improve over time.

4.5.2 Offer wider experiences

Physical conferences are limited to what happens in the conference centre during conference hours. Once you are liberated from the confines of a single space at a single time, you can become far more creative in your offerings. The STiR conference was organized so that attendees could do virtual site visits around the world and observe the programme in action. These site visits were set up to cater for different time zones. More stakeholders could attend each virtual site visit for three reasons:

- They could attend at a time that suited them.
- They did not have to travel halfway round the world to do a field visit.
- There was not the problem of having 40 'observers' crowding into a schoolroom to observe a lesson or a teacher meeting.

Being part of a live event, seeing the programme in action, is far more compelling than watching carefully choreographed videos which are, essentially, propaganda films. The live event is risky both technically and operationally: you cannot guarantee it will look perfect.

As soon as you go remote, the world becomes your playground

But it is far more engaging and effective. A remote event like this takes more, not less, preparation than an in-person event.

4.5.3 Attract the best speakers and experts

As soon as you go remote, the world becomes your playground. You are not limited to hiring a local speaker or expert so this is your chance to bring in genuinely fresh and original perspectives. Make the most of your opportunity.

4.5.4 Quicker, better, more focused break out groups

The Fair Education Alliance ran its annual conference for 150 of the most influential education organizations in the UK. Like many other organizations, they faced the challenge of moving a physical conference online. Here is how they managed to engage so many people for a two-day remote conference:

- *Break the conference up* into three-hour segments on different days: stakeholders could attend the conference but still do their day job. Attendance was high.
- *Move fast*: in physical conferences, attendees are a captive audience. Remotely, they are a click away from leaving, so keep the pace up. Keynote presentations are a hazard. Few people walk out of a conference hall, even if they are suffering death by PowerPoint. Online you have to work harder to keep engagement. Instead of a long monologue from the keynote speaker, organize an interview format in which the interviewer can moderate questions from attendees in real time via the chat function.
- *Break it up*. Frequent break out sessions ensured that everyone could make their voice heard and kept them engaged. Online, you can organize break out groups that last just 15 minutes, which is roughly the transition time required for a break out group at a physical conference.
- *Make it interactive*. Besides chat and break out sessions, use remote technology to do polls and engage opinion. Craft the polls so that you can generate real debate. A poll question asking 'is honesty good?' achieves

little. Asking 'Would you tell your colleague that their presentation was no good/they are dressed inappropriately for the occasion?' is a more provocative way of asking the same question and will generate a livelier response, if you want it.

- *Encourage chat.* Chat during a keynote speech at a physical conference is not good. Online chat during a conference works: attendees feel involved; they connect with each other and the organizers get real time feedback about what is working or not; the speaker is able to respond to questions and suggestions in real time. The speaker is not at the mercy of the loudmouth who decides to stand up and dominate the conference floor with a long-winded question at question time. Only the best questions survive, and only short questions are asked because loudmouths write less than they speak.

4.5.5 *Better mixing of participants*

In theory, and occasionally in practice, conferences allow people to network effectively. However, many company conferences fail in this respect. At the conference centre, each corporate tribe huddles together, based on their geography, seniority, business unit or function. In other words, too often people network with people they already know. Meanwhile a couple of VIPs get bombarded by strangers wanting a moment of their time, which means they then retreat to the safety of the VIP room to talk to other VIPs.

Online, you can organize break out groups to force people to mingle with people they will not know. This has to be done carefully. You have to think of yourself as a matchmaker organizing a series of dates: who needs to meet whom, and who wants to meet whom? Do the matchmaking well, and you will have very happy attendees; do it poorly and you may suddenly find that many of your attendees are suffering internet problems and are no longer online. The strongest form of feedback you receive is at the bottom of the screen, where it shows how many people are attending and you can see how many have dropped off.

These break outs can be for problem solving and work or they can be overtly for networking. Either way, keep them short. These should be speed dates that keep energy levels high. If successful, attendees can send private messages to each other after the break out group has finished.

> **Too often, people network with people they already know**

4.5.6 *Better use of time*

Physical conferences are anchored in a place, which means that they are also anchored in time. The conference is limited by the time the conference room is available, by check out times of the hotel and by check in times for flights. Going remote removes these time shackles from your conference. You can make the most of remote time in two ways.

- Split the conference into sections over different days, and possibly over different time zones. This makes it easier for key stakeholders to attend. They do not have to travel and they do not have to lose a day of work. Two half-days of a conference are likely to be more productive than one whole day stuck in an airless conference room. The half-days keep energy levels up and allow people to stay on top of their day job.
- Have frequent break outs. In a physical conference each break out is very time consuming: participants

ask questions about their assignment, go to get a coffee, go to the rest room, chat to someone in the corridor, get lost and can't find their room and finally make themselves comfortable. A remote break out can happen in seconds as attendees are automatically dropped into their virtual break out rooms. This makes it easier to have more frequent short and sharp break outs where you can do more productive work and you can organize more networking.

4.5.7 Lower cost

Lower cost may well be the long-term driver of more virtual conferences. Remote conferences save on flights, hotels, meals, bar bills, conference rooms, technicians and all the other expenses of a physical conference. And there is also lower opportunity cost as people spend less time travelling. But the benefit of lower cost is a trap; if remote conferences are simply cheap, then they will be useless. The challenge is to make them at least as good as physical conferences. Making a good remote conference work takes at least as much time as making a physical conference work. Re-invest some of the savings from the physical conference in making the remote conference a first class event: organize the best speakers and best inputs from around the world; surprise and delight attendees.

Although remote conferences are cheaper than live conferences, you still have to invest in them to make them work well:

- It is harder and takes more time to plan for interaction than to plan for a speech: interaction increases complexity and uncertainty.
- The technology has to work, and you have to rehearse it. It should feel slick, seamless and professional.

- Even when the technology works, many attendees will need help getting online because they have lost the login details, their technology does not work or they have misread the instructions. You need an easily accessible help hotline.
- Preparing videos, virtual field visits or virtual interviews with VIPs is a huge drain of effort.

In a truly hybrid world, conferences will become a mix of virtual and physical. There are still advantages to physical conferences that virtual conferences cannot replicate, yet. All the research shows that trust is very hard to build online. The chance to meet people properly face to face is a chance to build genuine trust by getting to know each other properly. Online conferences tend to be transactional: it is hard to replicate the quiet walk around the grounds or the drink in the bar where you can talk about life, not just talk about work. This magic of mingling is what will keep the conference circuit alive.

Trust is very hard to build online

4.6 Make meetings work

Why meetings are harder in a hybrid work era
Even in the era before the pandemic, meetings were problematic. They could be a waste of time and irrelevant. Even when they were useful and relevant, it could be hard to achieve the outcome you wanted. Remote meetings double down on these problems. As with everything about remote working, the solution is that you have to be much more purposeful and deliberate about attending and holding meetings. This is good news. The disciplines you acquire in holding effective remote meetings will enable you to hold far more productive in-person meetings.

Remote meetings are harder as a result of two root causes. On remote meetings it is harder to:

- Read body language.
- Build trust.

Teams which are well established can overcome these problems, because they have established bonds of trust and because each team member knows how everyone else behaves. We can predict their behaviour accurately, and that creates certainty and safety. The problems become more acute when you introduce different players into the meeting. They might be new joiners, or they might be people from other departments and functions. The bonds of trust are not so strong and we are much less able to predict behaviour: this leads to anxiety and tension.

This section looks at how you can make remote meetings work for you, as follows:

1. The body language challenge.
2. Zoom doom: escaping death by video meeting.
3. Before you start: set yourself up for success.
4. Introductions: starting meetings well.
5. Making the meeting work (as participant *and* as chairperson or host).
6. Closing the meeting.
7. Special situations: hybrid and global meetings.

4.6.1 *The body language challenge*

There is a beautiful and natural choreography to in-person meetings. We all read body language easily; it is as natural as breathing. It is so natural that we do not notice it, until it goes wrong. This is not about trying to pick up micro-expressions to see if someone is misleading us. It is much simpler. We read body language for three reasons:

- To see if others are paying attention or losing interest.
- To see who wants to speak next.
- To enhance our understanding of what is being said.

There are four main sorts of body language, plus eye contact, which you will naturally use to achieve these goals:

1. *Battle gestures*. We conduct the rhythm of our speech with our hands. But on video we become talking heads and we do not use battle gestures. This is a problem because people are prediction machines; we want to predict what is happening next. Prediction is about survival; our ancestors always needed to predict what that movement or noise in the long grass meant. Our ancestors who predicted that the noise in the long grass was a cuddly kitty were more likely to die out than those who predicted it could be a ravenous lion. Humans have learned to predict negatively, not positively. Battle gestures help us predict what is going to happen next. If we cannot predict what is going to happen next, we default to negative predictions.

2. *Illustrative gestures* which illustrate what we are saying. For instance, if we say 'this is high and this is low' we might use our hands to illustrate the point. This makes it easier for everyone to understand what is being said. When we have insufficient data to interpret what is happening we will default to negative bias. When we cannot predict, we become frustrated. This is why hearing halfalogues on public transport are so irritating: we naturally want to predict and complete the other half of the stranger's phone conversation, but we only hear one side of it.

3. *Self-soothing gestures*. This is when we smooth our hair or our clothes, or stroke our face. Often this is all you see of people when they are online and it is a classic sign of anxiety. So this means that the person is anxious and that makes everyone else more anxious. Anxiety, like laughter and COVID-19, is contagious. Because you normally only see heads on screen, you see the anxiety ripple across the screen as everyone starts self-soothing their hair and stroking their faces.

4. *Moderator signals* show who is talking; when we are ready to talk; when we are ready to be interrupted; and when we are not wanting to be interrupted. Unfortunately these signals are not cross-cultural. That means in a foreign country you may not get a word in because you will not understand the moderator signals. It also means that online we do not know how to get a word in and that raises anxiety.

5. *Eye contact*. You know when someone is paying attention to what you are saying because they look at you. When they start looking away or down at their notes, you have lost them. And when you want to speak, you will probably sit up a bit straighter to make yourself bigger and lean slightly across the table. You may look at the chair of the meeting to 'catch his eye': when he sees you, you will know that you are going to be called to speak. If none of that works, you may up the ante further and raise a finger, cough slightly or look more intensely at the speaker. If none of that works, the speaker is deliberately ignoring you and the tension around the table will rise. Everyone knows the rules of the game, even if they are not written down, and everyone knows when the rules are being broken.

The power of eye contact became clear to me when I was interviewing the owner of a restaurant chain over breakfast. He sat at his favourite table, where he could see the entire restaurant. As we were talking, I noticed his eyes were darting around. His eyes told me I did not have his 100 per cent attention. It

People want to predict what is happening next

was disconcerting enough that I asked him what was going on. He said: 'I can see that a customer at table 15 is getting agitated because she is not being served, so I have just told a waiter to go there immediately'. He'd told the waiter to go and attend to the customer without saying a word or making a gesture: it was all in the power of eye contact. His waiters had learned it was smart to keep one eye on the boss and do what his eyes told them to do.

In the course of this chapter you will discover how to overcome the body language and eye contact challenge on video calls. Two useful principles are:

- Position your camera so that your hand gestures can be seen. If you are too close to the camera you become a talking head and all your body language is lost; if you are too far from the camera then you become a dot on other people's screens.
- Position your camera so that you can look straight into it. This is hard to do. When we look at the screen we naturally look at the most interesting thing on the screen: our own face. After that, we might look at the speaker. In either case, the speaker will see that we are looking away from her. That is disconcerting for her, because it tells her that we are not engaged with what she is saying. She only knows that you are looking at her when you look straight down the camera.

4.6.2 *Zoom doom: escaping death by video meeting*

WFH meetings have not only become a substitute for work, they have squeezed out work. In the office, everyone knows you are (probably) working because they can see you at your hot desk. WFH, no one can see you working, and you probably do not want your video on permanently to let your boss see what you are doing. Video meetings let you show that you are at work but this can go too far. Senior executives can schedule their whole day with back-to-back meetings. This looks impressive in the diary, but is ineffective because it:

- Allows no time for thinking, analysing, reviewing or preparing: everything is about reacting in real time to someone else's agenda.
- Leads to stress and burnout: the absence of breaks in work is not sustainable. This has been known for over 100 years. You need short breaks once an hour to keep fresh and stay at the top of your game.

You need a way of deciding which meetings you should attend, and when you should host a meeting yourself. Each meeting you attend or host

You need short breaks once an hour

should pass three tests for you:

- What will I contribute?
- What will I learn?
- What will I do, or persuade others to do, as a result of the meeting?

Ideally, every meeting should pass all three tests. If you attend a meeting where you have learned nothing, contributed nothing and do nothing differently as a result, you will have just wasted an hour of your life which you cannot get back again. Here are the three tests in more detail:

- *What will I contribute?* If you contribute nothing, other attendees will wonder why you were there. They will assume that you have nothing useful to contribute. If that happens repeatedly, you start to earn an unhelpful reputation. Saying nothing is not a neutral activity: it is damaging to you and your career prospects. Too many meetings are full of hangers-on who want face time with senior people, but senior executives are not impressed with staff who have nothing to say and nothing to contribute.

  Your contribution does not have to be world changing. It can be about providing a point of view, relevant information or a different perspective. Occasionally, you can come up with these perspectives in real time as you react to the unfolding conversation. But if you want to be sure of making a contribution that gets noticed, plan in advance. Review the agenda beforehand and be ready with your point of view and the data to back it up. Do not stick 100 per cent rigidly to this, because the conversation may evolve in unexpected ways. Be prepared to customize your thoughts to the reality of the situation. If you are well prepared you will be able to adapt with ease.

  If there is nowhere for you to make a contribution, you may want to think about whether you need to be at the meeting. And if someone else, like your boss, can make the same points then how will you add any more value?

- *What will I learn?* Occasionally, you will look at an agenda and realize that you cannot contribute anything but you can learn a lot. You might learn about some upcoming new initiatives or organizational changes which present you with opportunities. Perhaps you will learn something new about the market from a meeting with customers or suppliers. These are useful meetings to attend, but dangerous. If you turn up to a customer meeting to learn from them, but have nothing to contribute back, the customer will not be impressed. Do not go to these meetings in the hope that you might learn something; only go if you see an agenda item absolutely relevant to you and you know you need to learn more. If it is genuinely relevant, then the chances are that the meeting will pass at least one of the other two tests of a meeting: either you will be able to contribute something, or you will do something different as a result of the meeting.

- *What will I do, or persuade others to do, as a result of the meeting?* Ultimately, meetings need to lead to some form of action. Either you need to do something, or you need to persuade someone else to do something, by the end of the meeting. This might be about agreeing or challenging a formal agenda item relevant to you. But many times the real action of the meeting takes place around its fringes: before the start and at the end. This is your chance to bump into ('accidentally') a hard to reach colleague and either reach a quick informal agreement, or to outline a challenge and set up a separate formal meeting to discuss it. If your only reason for attending a meeting is to meet someone around its fringes, make sure you find some way of making a contribution to the formal agenda. This is your chance to be constructive and supportive, and to make friends and allies. Save your fighting contributions, when you want to challenge something, for when you need to fight a battle on an agenda item which matters to you directly.

You can use these three tests when you want to host a meeting. The first question to ask is 'what will I do, or persuade others to do, as a result of the meeting?' This frames your goal for the meeting and will help you identify who needs to attend the meeting. Even if it **Meetings need to lead to some form of action** is an information sharing meeting where the focus is on 'what will I learn?' you should think about potential actions arising. Information is not an end in itself: it is a light that points the way to action.

The three tests will let you identify who needs to be at the meeting. For each person who attends you should be able to see that they will have productive answers to at least one, and ideally all three questions:

- What will I contribute?
- What will I learn?
- What will I do, or persuade others to do, as a result of the meeting?

These tests are simple to use. You do not need to hold a one-hour Zoom meeting to answer the questions. You can answer them in a couple of minutes while you are between other activities. It is a simple way of increasing your productivity. Using these three tests will allow you to:

- Have fewer meetings.
- Have more effective meetings.
- Invite the right people to your meetings.

4.6.3 *Before you start: set yourself up for success*
The military aphorism that 'if you fail to plan, plan to fail', rings true. If you take time to review the three tests of a meeting

(above) you are halfway to success. There is one other thing you can do to set yourself up for success: make sure you make a good first impression.

First impressions count, in person and online. It may take anything from two to ten seconds for those vital first impressions to form. In person, we make a good first impression by the way we enter the room, greet people and dress. Online we have different ways of making a good impression. Online first impressions are about how we look and how our background looks. WFH we are inviting people into our space, our house. You can make this work for your advantage. The neutral space of the office does not lend itself to intimacy, instead it leads to formality and emotional distance.

WFH it is tempting to recreate the business look of the office. This is where you either use a very neutral background which gives nothing away, or you use an office backdrop that you can load on to your video calling app. But why create distance with your colleagues when you can create closeness and warmth?

'If you fail to plan, plan to fail'

There are plenty of ways in which you can build intimacy very quickly and effectively online and even better than you can offline. You can achieve a level of proximity which is not possible offline. Here are some of the things you can do:

- Place things in the background which people can ask about. That leads to personal disclosure and the chance of making a human connection, not just a business connection. Disclosure is usually mutual: when you disclose something of yourself, your colleague will reciprocate. This is your chance to discover mutual interests which you would not discover by sitting in a functional meeting room. You can decide what you want to disclose in your background: you are in control. The background can be a mix of personal and professional interests.

- You can use your background to signal comfort. A sofa and cushions in the background signals 'home' and safety. Sometimes, meeting rooms can feel like gladiatorial arenas. The prospect of a potential gladiatorial fight with cushions is not threatening. You are more likely to have a productive meeting when colleagues feel relaxed and safe than when they are in fight or flight mode.
- Drinking coffee at the start of the meeting shows that you are comfortable. If you are comfortable, your colleagues are more likely to relax and feel comfortable. This is the mirror image of in-person meetings starting with everyone grabbing a coffee. But be careful: drinking coffee during an online meeting looks like you are disengaged.
- A well-lit background indicates a welcoming house that is occupied as opposed to a dark house that is threatening.

The home look still has to be professional, clean, quiet and tidy. If you look like you live amidst chaos, first impressions will be negative and probably accurate: chaos at home is likely to be reflected by chaos at work. And make sure that your workspace is quiet. In the early days of the pandemic it was cute to see toddlers and pets photobombing a video call. Now it is just a nuisance. Your working space may create the sense of home and comfort, but you still need clear boundaries between home and work.

You need clear boundaries between home and work

Not everyone has the luxury of a space at home that is quiet and suitable for conference calls. Coffee shops are not a suitable alternative, because there are far too many distractions and no confidentiality. Either you need to go into the office, or convince your employer to fund a local co-working space for you. Even here you may be able to add one or two personal touches to create a point of interest and welcome for your colleagues.

4.6.4 Introductions: starting meetings well

The most important part of many meetings are before they start and after they end. This is where vital and informal business is conducted. In many video meetings, participants simply disappear at the end, which makes the start even more important.

Before the formal start of in-person meetings, two things happen which help meetings succeed:

- Social alignment.
- Business alignment.

Social alignment is about building or reconfirming trust and personal connections. This is the apparently pointless social chit-chat before the meeting, perhaps as people pour themselves a coffee. But the simple act of greeting and making eye contact has a powerful effect. It says: 'we are friends or allies and we can work together.' We are not just social animals, we are tribal animals. When we leave our territory (our desk) and go to alien territory (a meeting room) we are no longer in a safe space. Finding allies and friends helps. If you look at who socializes with who before a meeting, you discover that it is not random. There is a clear pattern: potential allies chat to each other and reconfirm their connections. Potential rivals who might fight over an agenda item avoid each other, unless they decide to do some business before the meeting: that leads to the business alignment element of the pre-meeting time.

Online, social alignment can be as simple as greeting each person on the call. If you are chair, get on to the call two minutes early. This is a good investment of a little time because then you can greet each person as they log on to the call. If they have set up their backgrounds, that may even give you an opportunity to compliment them or ask them about something they have put on display. As you do your greetings, other attendees will start greeting each other as well. This is not as rich as in-person social alignment, but it is a start.

We are not just social animals, we are tribal animals

Business alignment does what it says on the tin. Pre-meeting time is your last chance to broker a deal, or at least a truce, on a contentious agenda item. It is also your chance to influence the chair, to make sure you get to speak when you need to. If you see potential rivals talking before the meeting, they are unlikely to be talking about cats and dogs: after a perfunctory social greeting they will set about their business.

All of this happens very fast and can make a big difference to how the meeting goes. Junior people who most need to get some social and business alignment will often be first to arrive, in the hope of meeting people who can offer moral or practical support. If you are very powerful you can make a statement by arriving late: you are powerful enough that you do not need to waste your time with pre-meeting niceties.

Business alignment is impossible to do at the start of an online meeting, because those discussions have to be private and personal. If there is an agenda item that is going to be contested, then identify the colleagues who will be on the other side of the debate. Reach out to them and have a separate call beforehand because it is easier to resolve differences in private than in public. Once a colleague takes a position in public, they will find it hard to climb down. In private, they can be more flexible.

4.6.5a Making the meeting work, as a participant

Imagine what would happen if, during an in-person meeting, a colleague never made eye contact with anyone, slouched,

If you attend a meeting, attend it properly

spent the meeting texting and sending emails and finally put a bag over her head so that no one could see her face.

It would not be acceptable in person and it is not acceptable online. If you attend a meeting, attend it properly.

If a meeting matters, show that it matters by engaging and paying attention. If the meeting does not matter, do not attend. Here is how you can show you are engaged online:

- *Make eye contact.* During in-person meetings eye contact is vital. It not only shows you are listening, it helps you listen by making you focus on the speaker and not on your notes or instant messages. Set up your computer and camera so that you can look down the camera lens. If your screen is to one side of your camera you will never look like you are engaged.
- *Sit up straight.* This makes you look like you are paying attention and it helps keep your energy levels up. When you slouch, energy levels and attention levels slouch as well.
- *Smile occasionally.* This shows you are listening and reacting, and is a good way to maintain social alignment with others on the call: you are giving your approval to the speaker. The speaker will then feel obliged to reciprocate your favour when you speak later on.
- *Do not turn off your video.* That is the equivalent of putting a bag over your head during an in-person meeting. It shows that you are checking out and doing emails, feeding the dog or practising the ukulele. In the

early days of the pandemic you could pretend that your internet connection was unstable but now, there are no excuses.

When you want to speak you have to sell the fact that you want to speak. With in-person meetings this is easy: your body language will tell everyone that you want to speak, and the rhythm of the conversation will let you start. Online, others cannot read your body language and it is harder to judge the rhythm of the conversation. Do not be subtle: raise a finger to show you want to come in, and then raise a hand. Unmute yourself to signal you are ready to speak, and so that you do not annoy everyone else by being inaudible when you start to talk.

When you have a chance to speak, use it well. Unlike in-person meetings, you will find it hard to judge the reaction of your colleagues because you will not be able to read their body language. You will not be able to correct course in response to how colleagues are reacting. This means you need to be more prepared, more deliberate and more purposeful in what you say. You need to sell your idea:

- *Keep it short and focused.* Long interventions are unhelpful during in-person meetings, but at least you have a captive audience. Online, colleagues will simply tune out unless you can grab them and keep them engaged.
- *Make it relevant.* The goal of speaking is not to listen to your own voice. Be clear about the problem you are identifying, the solution you have or the support or perspective you are offering. If you have neither a problem nor a solution, nor support or perspective, you are probably adding nothing to the discussion.
- *Support assertions with facts*, which should be short, simple and memorable. If you say something is

important, strategic, difficult or impossible, you need to show why. One killer fact is more powerful than a complex spreadsheet, because people can remember a killer fact better than they can remember a complex spreadsheet. You need to be well prepared to have the right facts to hand.

- *Keep the end in mind.* Know what outcome you want to achieve as a result of your intervention. If you simply want to look smart by saying something clever, shut up. If you are going to derail an agenda item, take care. Sometimes it is better to win a friend than to win an argument: it is easier to resolve differences between friends than between adversaries.
- *Use hand gestures.* Talking heads are tiring and boring because of the lack of body language. Make sure your camera allows people to see you communicate with your hands. It is more engaging and more powerful than a talking head.
- *Speak well.* Consider your tone of voice, which can be very business-like or very warm. In the absence of body language, tone of voice is essential in conveying your intentions. Warmth is disarming and defuses tension. The difference is in the length of your vowels: longer vowels are warmer. Try saying 'welcome everyone' briskly with short vowels and then slowly with long vowels. The brisk version says 'Let's cut through the nonsense and get down to business', the long version is a genuine welcome. You can use both styles to your advantage.

There are some people who can do all of this naturally and in real time. For the other 99 per cent of us, this means that we have to prepare carefully beforehand. Know where you want to make an impact on the agenda and know how you are going to make an impact. On less important items you can still talk on the spur of the moment: stick to the principles above and you are likely to have more impact than less prepared colleagues.

It is better to win a friend than to win an argument

4.6.5b Making the meeting work, as the chairperson or host
In some ways, chairing an online meeting is easier than chairing an in-person meeting:

- Attendees turn up on time, which allows the meeting to start on time.
- Attendees tend to be politer: they are less likely to interrupt and talk over each other.
- It is harder for one person to dominate discussion. In-person meetings are often hijacked by the person with the biggest mouth, greatest ego and most confidence. Online they find it harder to interrupt, and it is harder to sustain a speech online in the absence of any oral or body language feedback.

The normal disciplines of agenda management and discussion management apply online. There are two areas requiring special attention online.

- *Make a good start.* Arrive two minutes before the scheduled start of the meeting so that you can greet everyone. It is also a good moment to ask if anyone has any other business they want to add to the agenda. This allows you to manage time better and it also means the person with the extra agenda item can relax and will not be trying to squeeze the point in earlier by hijacking an existing agenda item.

- *Manage the discussion.* Online it is easy to spot who has spoken and who has kept quiet. Make a habit of asking each person if there is anything they want to add to the discussion on an agenda item, and make it clear that it is fine for them simply to agree with what has already been said. Doing this consistently gives all attendees structure and certainty: they know they will be asked to speak, so they do not have to worry about forcing their way into the discussion. This reduces their anxiety and it also means that they will not feel the need to interrupt. They can relax, safe in the knowledge that they will have their turn. It also means that they have to stay alert and pay attention: they may be asked to speak at any time. The order in which you ask people to speak will reflect how relevant the agenda item is, and where the expertise lies around the table.

4.6.6 *Closing the meeting*

Finish well. Aim to finish 10 minutes before the scheduled finish. If you finish 10 minutes early, everyone will be grateful for having a break between meetings. It also gives you time to deal with any overruns.

Close by summarizing any key points, agreements or actions. This is the time to identify and deal with any misunderstandings. Making the agreements and actions public now forces anyone with reservations to speak up. The discussion should be closed by the end of the meeting. This is vital in online meetings. If there is a disagreement about outcomes in the office, you can normally resolve it quickly and informally by talking to the person who disagrees, but when they disagree online, it can quickly blow up into a storm of emails and instant messages which only get resolved by another formal meeting.

The meeting is not completely finished until it is documented. That is when the agreements and actions are formally recognized.

Online, this is particularly important: many colleagues will be suffering meeting overload and find it hard to keep track of what was agreed by whom, when and where. Documentation can be as simple as a message to everyone thanking them for coming and covering two or three key points; this can and should be sent out within an hour of the meeting finishing. More formal meetings require more formal minutes. A good discipline is the 24-hour rule: minutes should reach everyone within 24 hours of the meeting ending. This works because it:

- Is easier to write minutes while the meeting is fresh in your mind.
- Ensures attendees know what they need to do next in a timely manner.
- Demonstrates competence, which enhances your credibility.

4.6.7a Special situations: Hybrid meetings

Not all meetings are created equal: some are harder than others. Hybrid meetings present special challenges. Many people have tried hybrid meetings and few have succeeded. The only

Not all meetings are created equal

people who think they work are the people who are in the office; remote attendees normally leave the meeting frustrated.

Hybrid meetings create two classes of attendee. In-person attendees can see each other; they have the social alignment, they can work the agenda informally, they can read each other's body language and it is easy for them to carry on the conversation and more or less disregard the online attendees. Meanwhile, the online attendees, because they feel excluded, find it hard to intervene and they cannot read anyone's body language: attendees in the office appear as little more than blobs on the screen.

Firms have found three solutions to this problem.

1. Avoid holding hybrid meetings. This is simple, ingenious and it works, unless you have half the team in the office and half outside. Then you have to resort to option two.
2. Replicate the online experience. This solution requires everyone in the office to retreat to separate rooms and log into the call as if they were attending online. This appears cumbersome, but it ensures a level playing field between all the attendees.
3. Attempt to run the meeting in hybrid fashion. Two simple actions help in this case. First, insist that the in-person attendees all login separately, even if they are sitting at the same table. This gives remote attendees a better chance of reading body language and understanding what is going on. Second, always ask the remote attendees to comment first on an agenda item. This keeps them involved and ensures that airtime is not monopolized by the in-person attendees.

4.6.7b Special situations: Global meetings
Global teams are remote teams on steroids. Everything is harder on a global team and the challenge increases as differences in time zones, language and culture increase. Even when global meetings are held in person, the language and cultural challenges are obvious. In such a meeting, see who talks the most. There is a predictable hierarchy when it comes to share of voice:

- Americans usually have the highest market share: they are native speakers and they are culturally attuned to the idea that you should be an active participant in a meeting. Saying nothing implies that you have nothing to say: it is a sign of weakness.

- Other native English speakers and Europeans tend to have the next highest share of voice: they are linguistically confident; they may give space for others to speak which means that they do not dominate, but they expect to speak out themselves.

- Some (not all) Asian cultures have near zero share of voice. This is sometimes embarrassment about speaking a language in which they are not confident about being fluent. Sometimes it is cultural hesitancy: either there is respect for hierarchy or a distaste for disagreement in public.

Each participant is acting in a culturally appropriate way, but the result is a completely unbalanced meeting. Online, the imbalance is even greater

Saying nothing implies that you have nothing to say

with attendees from the host country typically gaining a disproportionate share of voice.

Research on global teams shows that the two biggest challenges, which are closely linked, are trust and communications. Here is how different firms deal with the challenges of trust and communications across cultures on global meetings:

- Meet face to face. Every global team finds that the quality of interaction rises dramatically after teams have met in person. Mutual understanding, respect and trust rises, which makes for easier communication. Remote meetings work better after face-to-face meetings. This is the single most important thing you can do to make global meetings work.

- Build culturally homogenous teams. This is the 'empire' form of global firm which operates with a pyramid of passports: nearly all of the top executives come from the home country of the global firm; below that come managers from the 'West'; at the bottom the people doing the dirty, dull or dangerous work come from emerging economies. This is more comfortable for the people at the top than at the bottom. A cohesive culture at the top is good for ensuring mutual understanding, but inevitably makes it hard to recruit top talent locally. Top talent from other countries does not want to join a firm that operates a pyramid of passports, because they know that they are barred from the top of the pyramid. A soft version of this is to have diversity of passports, but from a similar cultural background: Anglophone countries work together and European countries work together.
- Build global teams on the same time zone. Some US IT firms outsource mainly to South America; some European firms outsource to South Africa and Australian firms outsource to the Philippines. This does not deal with the cultural issue, but at least it removes the time zone problem and makes frequent communication easier.
- Force teams to use written communication, not meetings. Written communication has several advantages in a global team:
  - It avoids misunderstanding.
  - Asynchronous communication reduces the time zone problem.
  - It prevents one culture dominating share of voice: every voice can be heard.

  The main problems with written communications are:
  - Writing takes time and requires discipline to achieve clarity and accuracy.

- It is not good when you need a discussion to solve a problem.
- Picking up the phone is often quicker and simpler.

4.7 Key points

1. Set your team up for WFH success: home office set up should be as professional as in-office set up.
   - Set clear goals because presenteeism does not equal productivity at home or the office.
2. Re-engineer the office: different spaces for solo work, formal meetings and collaboration.
3. Develop daily rhythms and routines: deliver productivity and work-life balance.
   - Agree core and flexible hours for WFH.
   - Agree when your team is in or out of the office.
   - Morning YTH meeting to kick start and co-ordinate the day.
4. Create your own team success charter: the Methods Adoption Workshop.
   - Brainstorm working method; stress test with critical incidents; review and repeat regularly.
5. Re-imagine virtual conferences:
   - Replicating physical conferences fails.
   - Virtual conferences allow you to be different and better: wider participation, global experts, more convenient timings, more efficient break out sessions, easier participation and contribution.
6. Online meetings suffer trust and communication problems with little body language. Take extra effort to make your online meeting work:
   - Set up your background to invite people into your space: create intimacy remotely.

- Only attend a meeting if you can contribute something, learn something and do something different as a result of the meeting.
- Prepare your interventions so that they are crisp, relevant and effective.
- Make your language and your body language work online.

Conclusion: the new world of Smart Work

*'There are decades when nothing happens and
weeks when decades happen.'*

V.I. Lenin

The COVID-19 pandemic has changed the nature of leadership and work for good, and for better. It has certainly accelerated trends which were already there: more trust, delegation, autonomy, accountability and less micromanagement. Inevitably, there will be winners and losers, and the winners will be those who adapt fastest and best to the new world. Those who try to stick with what worked before will find their comfort zone becomes increasingly uncomfortable in the new world. We all have to learn, change and raise our game.

We all have to learn, change and raise our game

The Smart Work revolution is only just beginning. In years to come, we will see the pandemic as a dividing line between the old way of doing things and the new way of doing things. There is no going back to the old ways. Smart Work is a permanent revolution:

- *The stigma of working from home (WFH) has gone.* WFH used to be seen as SFH: 'Shirking From Home'. But employers and employees have found that productivity is more likely to rise with WFH. If you work from home now, you are no longer an outlier: you are part of the new normal.

- *WFH reduces costs for employer and employee*. Employers will reduce their need for office space, and therefore their rent, and travel budgets are likely to be slashed. Employees will spend less on commuting, meals, dry cleaning and all the other incidentals of work.
- *Employees want WFH for 2–3 days per week*. This is a universal finding across sectors and across geographies. Even in Japan, where homes really are not set up for WFH, people want to work from home for 2–3 days a week: perhaps the joy of long commutes on packed trains wears off after the first 20 years or so.
- *The investment in WFH has been made*: back-end and home working systems have been created, so that there is no longer any investment barrier to WFH. Helping an extra employee to work remotely can now be done at marginal cost.
- *Network effects amplify all these changes*. It can be hard for one firm to move to WFH. But when the whole system moves to WFH, it becomes the new normal to meet, chat and interact virtually.
- *The pandemic forced experimentation*, which would never have happened before. Experimentation has led to solutions that demonstrably work. We are only at the start of this revolution, and the solutions will only improve over time.

There is a dark side to all revolutions and Smart Work is no exception:

- *Mental health has suffered*. The silver lining is that employers may finally start to treat mental health as seriously as physical health at work. The return to the office on a part-time basis will greatly alleviate this problem.

- *The pandemic has been divisive.* If you have a good home working environment and are established in your role, you are part of the COVID aristocracy. Many lower-paid, frontline workers have no WFH option. Employees new to the workforce often have unsuitable home working conditions, and will need the office for support, mentoring, culture, structure and social contact.

- *The dark side of more autonomy is more accountability.* WFH gives you more freedom and control, which means fewer excuses for not performing. It is not enough to perform well; you have to show that you perform well even when your team and bosses cannot see you.

- *WFH can be risky for your career.* Limited research shows that in firms where there is a mix of office and WFH, office-based workers are three more times likely to be promoted. WFH allows more flexible working hours which should help attract a more diverse workforce, but the pull of the office when it comes to promotions works against diversity. The old rule still applies: if you want a job, WFH; if you want a career go to the office.

- *WFH is also risky for your job.* Employers no longer need to recruit locally for the office. They can recruit the best talent at the lowest cost from wherever they want. You may now have to compete with a much greater talent pool than ever before.

- *Smart Work will create winners and losers.* Not all staff, leaders and firms will manage the transition successfully. This book is your guide to coming out on the winning side of the revolution.

The dark side of Smart Work should be temporary, as firms start to discover solutions to each of these challenges. We are at the start, not the end, of the Smart Work revolution. It is a revolution which carries with it the huge promise of a better future in which:

Smart Work will create winners and losers

- *Staff can find a better work-life balance*, with more flexible working and greater diversity.
- *Leaders and managers will have to raise their game.* They will have to become more purposeful and deliberate in how they lead: everyone benefits from better management.
- *We will finally arrive in the world of twenty-first-century work.* Professionals will have to be treated like professionals: more trust, more delegation and more autonomy than ever before.
- *We will use the office less but more effectively*: for communication, team building, mentoring, collaborating, problem solving and creating a common culture.

As has been said, the pandemic did not cause the revolution: it has simply accelerated trends which were already there. The deeper currents that will continue to propel the revolution include:

- *Education:* today's professional has to be managed differently from the more unskilled labour force of 200 years ago. Command and control is giving way to influence and motivation.
- *The nature of work is becoming more ambiguous.* It is easy to measure the quantity and quality of widget production, for example, but much harder to assess the output of professional work, especially where it is office based.

- *Power is shifting from employer to employee.* The days of the one-company town have been consigned to history. As the war for talent heats up, employers and leaders are losing their coercive power. Leaders need to become the leader people *want* to follow, not the leader they *have* to follow.
- *Technology enables the revolution*, even if it has not caused it: smart work simply would not have been possible in the 1980s, before the advent of the internet and personal computing.

Progress has always been uneven and the future will arrive in different places at different times. Some firms will embrace the new world. Others will use technology to create a 'back to the future' dystopian world where technology controls rather than enables humans. Delivery workers, warehouse workers and many others have already discovered that, when your boss is an algorithm, your boss is a tyrant. Algorithms do not care about your stress, your tiredness,

The future will arrive in different places at different times

your domestic crisis: it simply wants the most output in the most efficient way. These high-tech tyrants take management back to the nineteenth century: technology can help us regress as well as progress.

The journey to the future is inherently unknowable, but the pandemic has opened up a glimpse of a future which has the potential to be far better than the past. Every firm and every individual will discover a different path to the future. Along the way you will have triumphs and disasters, joy and despair: that is the journey of every life. But whatever your journey is, enjoy it.

Acknowledgements

This book was a huge team effort. I would like to thank Ian Hallsworth and the team at Bloomsbury for taking on this project and for Ian's sound guidance throughout; Jason Bartholomew made the right things happen as my agent; and Mark Bowden was a helpful genius on body language. Steve Chase and the team at idAudio worked magic to help me turn the written word into the spoken word and the audiobook version of *Smart Work*.

So many people contributed their time and insight to this book it is impossible to recognize them all, but I would like to mention the following who went out of their way to help: Omar Al-Farsi, Sandie Bakowski, Patrick Brady, Adrian Dougherty, Vicky Grinnell-Wright, Russell Hobby, Patricia Lajara, Marco Maccari, Debra Medhurst, Luke Morini, Yasmine Morrison, Ilias Papakonstantinou, Ben Peachey, Emily Preston, Ken Rauch, Jane Royden, David Stephen, Magdalena Walawska-Nowak, Gosia Walendzik, Crispin White and Jo Youle.

Anyone who has enjoyed the doubtful delights of lockdown will know the vital importance of a supportive partner, and I am eternally grateful to my wife Hiromi for her support, endurance and understanding.

Appropriately, *Smart Work* has been created entirely remotely. I am hugely grateful to everyone who made it happen. And if there are any failings, they are all mine. Finally, my thanks to you for reading the book. I hope you find it useful and even enjoyable.

Index

accountability   9, 11, 19, 23–4, 54, 72, 99–104, 114, 133, 179
agendas, meeting   159–60, 165
anxiety   31, 54, 59, 67, 80, 100, 112, 113, 118, 133–4, 154, 156, 170
arguments   26, 37
    see also misunderstandings
assignment choice   49, 71–2, 111
asynchronous communication   32–3, 174
    see also email; instant messaging
autonomy   8, 11, 19, 53–4, 72, 99–104, 107, 114, 179, 180

bad bosses   14, 49, 54, 78, 108
body language   154–5, 176
    battle gestures   155
    eye contact   156
    hybrid meetings   171
    illustrative gestures   155
    moderator signals   156
    self-soothing gestures   156
bosses, reaching out to   83
braver leadership   2, 3
British Council   143
buddy systems   113
budget   20, 49, 59, 60, 68, 92, 103, 106, 107

'burning platforms'   64, 66
burnout   35, 102, 118, 127, 129, 130–2, 158

career management   48–9, 71–2
caring for your team   81
    see also supportive relationships
catastrophizing   83, 84–5, 114
CEO's agenda, aligning with   70
chairing/hosting remote meetings   169–71
chairs, office   125, 134
change, driving/sustaining   63–4, 72
    capacity and capability   65, 73
    fears   66–7
    first steps   65, 73
    in-office coalition building   69–70, 71
    individual perspective   67–8
    informal meetings   69–71
    internal competition for resources   68–9
    need for change   64–5, 73
    N+V+C+F>R   64–6
    risk   65–6, 73
    visible alignment with CEO   70
    vision for change   65, 73
    WFH coalition building   70–1

claims to fame, building 46–7, 49
clothing, work 39–40, 119
collaborative work 4, 11, 134,
    135, 136, 138, 180
  remote conferences 146–53
colleagues, reaching out to 83
command and control 1, 13,
    14–15, 18–19, 29, 53–4, 70,
    99, 180
commitment, gaining 29–34
commuting 118, 119
competing for credit 47–8
conferences, remote 146–7, 175
  break-out groups 149–52
  costs 152–3
  experience diversity 148
  inclusivity 147–8
  participant mixing 150–1
  speakers and experts 148–9,
    152
  technology 152–3
  use of time 151–2
counselling services 76
counting your blessings 85–6
COVID-19 global pandemic 1–2,
    4–5, 6, 7–8, 10–11, 53, 54,
    64–6, 91–2, 132, 177, 178
credibility, demonstrating 17,
    34–5, 50
  accidentally over-
    committing 37–8, 50
  acting the part 39–40, 50
  failing to say no 35–6, 50
  setting up for success 36–7,
    47, 49, 50
credit, claiming 47–8
crisis management 24–5, 45–6
criticism, impact of 26
cultural challenges, global
    meeting 172–4

deadlines, managing 87
decision makers, access to 71–2
decision making 6–7, 141
delegating work 19, 55–6, 72,
    180
  having the right team 56–7
  knowing how you can
    delegate 58–9
  knowing what you can
    delegate 57–8
difficult conversations 72
discovered vs revealed
    truth 146
discovery process, goal
    alignment 29–31, 34
diversity of passports, global
    team 174
divided workforce 179
dress codes 39–40

EBI - even better if? 109–11,
    114, 144–5
email communications 7, 19, 29,
    32–3, 59, 114, 129, 139, 141
emotional risk, reducing 42–3
energizer exercises 131–2
energy levels 122–5, 130–2,
    151, 166
enjoying your work 49
enlightened selflessness 18
excess communication 138
exercise, physical 80, 114, 119
expectations, managing 36–7,
    38–9
experience, learning from 108
  see also tacit knowledge
explicit knowledge, mastering
    104–5, 106, 114
extrinsic motivation 89
eye contact 156–7, 166

face-to-face meetings   3–4, 32,
    36, 44, 173
Fair Education Alliance   149–50
family and friends   83
Federal Express   92–3
Financial Times   142–3
first impressions   162
flat organizations   104
friends and family   83

gamification of praise   27
global teams/meetings   117,
    172–5
goal alignment   16–17, 50
    horizontal challenge
      - stakeholder
      commitment   32–4
    vertical challenge - team
      commitment   28, 29–31
goal clarity   80, 100–1, 103, 113,
    132–4
goal setting   7
goals, personal   91
gossip   46, 79, 95
graduate recruits   112

hand gestures *see* body
    language
health and safety   125–6
helping out   97–8
high concentration work   4, 11,
    136, 138
hobbies and interests   24–5
home working *see* hybrid
    working; meetings,
    remote; remote working
hot desking   134–5
Human Resources   71–2
hybrid meetings, holding
    successful   171–2

hybrid working   1, 2, 10–11,
    14–16, 72, 95, 104, 118
    budget and resource issues   20
    creating a network of
      influence   44–9, 51
    delegation   19
    demonstrating
      credibility   34–40, 50
    end of command and
      control   18–19
    goal alignment   28–34, 50
    managing risk   40–4, 51
    monitoring progress   19
    motivation   19
    new normal   178
    performance assessment   19
    quality assurance   19
    solving challenges   19
    understanding influence
      17–18
    understanding trust   16–17
    values alignment   20–8, 50
    what employees want   178

ideas/strategy   60
    characteristics of good
      ideas   61–2
    considering CEO focus   62–3
    story in three parts   60–1
in-person meetings   27–8, 32,
    43, 50
    see also face-to-face meetings;
      private meetings
induction programmes   112
Industrial Revolution   1
influence, creating a network of
    see network of influence
influencing people   6–7, 10,
    17–18
    see also network of influence

informal talks and meetings   6–7, 20, 29, 44, 67, 68, 69–70, 71, 72, 81–2, 95, 135
information flow   19, 45, 46, 47, 137
inner world management   81–8, 114
Innovation Unit   147
instant messaging   32–3, 129, 139, 141
internet connection   126
interruptions/distractions in work   121–2
intrinsic motivation   89
    see mini/motivation RAMP
IPM concept - Idea, People, Money and Machine   60
isolation, social   7, 11, 24, 76, 94
IT at home   126–7, 134, 141, 181

job crafting   91–3, 115

Kennedy, J.F.   61–2
key influencers/stakeholders, access to   69, 70, 71–2, 135
keyboard loggers   15
kindness   23–4
Kissinger, Henry   5

learning from experience   108
    see also tacit knowledge
listening skills   34, 50
location trackers   15

Machiavelli   14, 15
mastery of skills   104–13, 114
meeting schedules   124, 131
meetings, remote
    acknowledging agreements and actions   170–1

agendas   159–60, 165, 169
back-to-back meetings/Zoom doom   158–61
body language   154–7, 167, 169, 176
business alignment   165
camera position and status   157, 166–7
chairing/hosting   169–71
challenges in hybrid work era   153–4
choosing meetings to attend   158–61, 176
closing the meeting   170–1
coffee/tea   162
daily morning meetings   24, 31, 138–9, 141
discussion management   170
documentation   170–1
engaging as a participant   166–8
eye contact   156–7
first impressions   162–4
gauging your potential contribution   159
global teams   172–5
hybrid meetings   171–2
introductions/starting meetings well   164–5, 169
learning opportunities   159–60
lighting   163
office background   162–3, 175
opportunities to persuade/gain support   160–1
outcome focus   168
posture   166
relevant contributions   167, 175

short and focused
    contributions   167, 175
smiling   166
social alignment   164, 166
supporting facts   167–8
tone of voice   168, 176
trust issues   154
what employees want   178
workspace   162–4
your chance to speak   167–8
see also video conferencing
mental health issues   6, 10, 11,
    75–7, 81–4, 178–9
Methods Adoption
    Workshop   140–1, 175
    1. brainstorming/agree rules
        of engagement   141–2
    2. stress testing your
        answers   142–3
    3. review your progress
        and solutions after one
        month   143–5
    quarterly review   146
micromanagement   8, 14–15, 72
mini/motivation RAMP   90
    autonomy and accountability
        99–104, 114
    building supportive
        relationships   93–8, 114
    finding your purpose   91–3,
        115
    mastery for motivation   104–
        13, 115
Missing People charity   3
misunderstandings   7, 20, 23,
    35, 59, 88, 135, 170
see also problem solving
monitoring progress   19
morning meetings, daily   24,
    31, 138–9, 141

motivation   7, 11, 19, 75–7, 88
    autonomy and
        accountability   99–104,
        114
    building supportive
        relationships   93–8, 114
    catastrophizing   84–5, 114
    creating conditions to
        thrive   77–9, 114–15
    extrinsic motivation   89
    finding your purpose/job
        crafting   91–3, 115
    goal clarity   80, 100–1, 103
    helping out   97–8
    managing your inner
        world   81–8, 114
    mind reading vs
        enquiry   86–8
    mini/motivation RAMP
        90–113
    new joiners   111–13
    positive vs negative
        behaviour   78–9, 84–8
    reach out and listen   95, 114
    responding
        appreciatively   95–7
    rhythms and routines   78,
        79–80, 114
    rumination vs reaching
        out   82–3, 84–5
    setting up for success   100,
        101–2, 103–4, 114
    skills mastery   104–11

nemawashi   69
network of influence   17–18,
    44–5, 51, 151
    building a claim to fame
        46–7, 49, 51
    give to take   47–8, 51

going where the power
   is   48–9, 51
stepping up   45–6, 51
networks of trust   45, 70, 135
new team members/joiners
   41, 111–13, 145–6, 154
Nikkei   142–3
'no,' failing to say   35–6

office chairs   125, 134
office environment   4, 6–7, 8,
   11, 102
   acquiring tacit knowledge
      107–9, 111, 112–13, 115
   building coalitions   69–70,
      71, 180
   building influence   45
   career management/
      building   71–2, 179
   delegation   59
   demonstrating
      credibility   36, 38
   design of physical
      space   134–7, 175
   gaining commitment   30–1,
      33
   informal/corridor meetings
      6–7, 20, 29, 44, 67, 68–70,
      71, 72, 95, 109, 135
   intelligence gathering   69–70,
      71
   internal competition   68–9
   management vs
      leadership   54–5
   misunderstandings   20, 35,
      88, 135
   new joiners   111, 135
   private meetings   44, 69,
      70–1, 135
   'reading the air'   44

risk discussions   44, 67
team quality compromise
   57
online training   3–4, 106–7
open plan working   134–5
optimism vs pessimism   85
over-committing   35–6, 37–8, 50
overwork   9–10, 54, 100, 118,
   122, 128
ownership   23–4
   see also accountability

paraphrasing   87
peer praise   26–7
peer pressure   44
personal goals   91
persuading stakeholders/
   colleagues   32–4
persuasion vs influence   18
pessimism   85
phone conversations   32, 131
politics, organizational   69, 94,
   102, 105
Pomodoro technique   124–5
positive regard   22–3
positivity   78–9, 84–9
power shifts   8–9, 181
praise, giving   25–7, 47–8, 50,
   96–7
priorities, managing   102, 103
private meetings   32, 43, 44, 69,
   70, 71, 135
problem solving   7, 19, 23,
   32–3, 45–6, 135, 142, 151,
   180
product guarantees   41
productivity   120–1, 123, 125
professional regard   143
progression, employee   19–20
public meetings   27, 32

purpose, finding your   91–3, 115
pyramid of passports, global
    team   174

quality assurance   19
quiet zones, office   136

RACI analysis   142
RAMP framework   ix–xvi
    see also mini/motivation RAMP
recruitment   21–2
    see also new team members/
    joiners
remote meetings *see* meetings,
    remote
remote working   1, 2, 95
    acquiring new skills   8–10
    acquiring tacit
        knowledge   105, 109–11,
        115
    communicating and
        coordinating   6
    daily morning meetings   24,
        31, 138–9, 141
    decision making   141–2
    energy levels   122–5, 130–2
    goal setting and goal
        clarity   7, 132–4, 175
    influencing people and
        decision making   6–7
    IT at home   126–7
    loss of stigma   177–8
    managing less, leading
        more   54–9, 72, 180
    managing your inner
        world   81–2
    Methods Adoption
        Workshop   140–1, 175
    mind reading vs enquiry
        86–8

misunderstandings   59, 88,
    135, 170
morning meetings   24, 31, 175
motivating staff   7, 11
movement of
    information   19
new joiners   111–13
new normal   178
physical environment   125–6,
    134
productivity   120–1, 123,
    125, 132–4
purposeful and deliberate
    management   6–8, 180
reduced costs   178
results focus   99–100
rhythms and routines   79–80,
    120–2, 137–40, 141
setting up for success   118–37
time boundaries   77–8, 138,
    139–40, 141
tools/IT for the job   125–7,
    134, 141
training courses   106–7
video conferencing   32, 36,
    37, 59, 67, 69, 102, 123–4,
    126, 131, 138–9, 141 (*see
    also* meetings, remote)
virtual conferences   146–53,
    175
weak performance   57
work clothes   40, 119
work/life boundaries   118–20,
    127–30
workspace   120, 141, 162–4,
    175
resources   20, 36, 49, 68, 102
responding appreciatively   95–7
rest breaks   122–3, 130, 158
results focus   99–100

reviews, buyer 41
rhythms and routines 78, 79–80, 114, 120–2, 137–40, 141
risk management 17, 40–1, 51, 66–7
emotional risk 42–3
increasing risk 43–4
rational risk 41–2
risk-reward principle 33–4
role models 24–5, 50, 77–9, 108
routines 78, 79–80, 114, 120–2, 137–40
rumination vs reaching out 82–3, 85

short interval scheduling 124–5
skills, acquiring new 8–10, 49
skills mastery 104–13, 114
Slack channels 24, 27, 46, 95, 139
sleep deprivation 123
social bonding 28, 153, 164
social media 24, 27
see also Slack channels
social support, lack of 7, 24, 76
see also supportive relationships
solo work focus 11, 138, 139–40
speakers, virtual conference 148–9, 152
speed of adaptation 1, 2, 3, 10
stability, human need for 63–4, 72
staff, reaching out to 80
staff recruitment 21–2
stakeholder goal alignment 32
STiR Education 147, 148
stress 9, 10, 11, 54, 57, 59, 80, 100, 102, 103, 118, 122, 127, 133–4, 142, 158, 181

stress testing 87, 142–3
success formula, creating a 140–6
success, setting up for 47, 49, 100, 113, 114
you 36–7, 101–3, 118–27
your team 103–4, 127–37
see also meetings, remote
supportive relationships 11, 13, 24, 79, 93–8, 114
surveillance software 9, 15, 18, 181

tacit knowledge, acquiring 105, 107–11, 114
new joiners 111–13
talent pool, geographical increase in 179
Taylor, F.W. 122–3, 130
TeachFirst 3–4
team goal alignment 28, 29–31
team meetings see morning meetings, daily
team progression 19–20
technical/operational support 11
technical skills 104–5
telephone conversations 32, 131
thinking work 4, 11, 136, 138
'three blessings' exercise 85–6
time boundaries 77–8, 80, 107, 114, 128–30, 138, 139–40, 141
time zone issues 174
Timpson, John 21–2, 26
tit-for-tat collaboration 48, 97–8, 114
tone of voice 168, 176

training courses   106–7

trust   8–9, 15–17, 32, 34, 37,
    40–1, 45, 49, 50, 55–6, 57,
    95, 153, 180

value alignment   16, 20–1, 50, 142
  being a role model   24–5, 50
  hire to values   21–8, 50, 56
  meeting in person   27–8
  ownership/accountability
    23–4
  positive regard   22–3, 50
  reinforcing team values   25–8
video conferencing   32, 36, 37,
    59, 67, 69, 102, 123–4, 126,
    131, 138–9, 141
  see also meetings, remote;
    remote working

walking breaks/phone calls   80,
    119, 123, 131
welcome packages   112
WIFM factor   33

work-life balance/boundaries
    11, 76, 80, 114, 118–19,
    127–30, 135, 180
working from home (WFH)
    see hybrid working;
      meetings, remote;
      remote working
workload management   6, 103,
    128, 130, 135
workspace   120, 134–7, 141,
    162–4, 175
written communication
  advantages vs
    disadvantages   174–5
WWW - what worked
    well?   109–11, 114, 144

YTH meetings   138–9, 140,
    141, 175

Zoom calls see meetings, remote;
    remote working; video
    conferencing